Sunset
Dinner Party Cook Book

By the Editors of *Sunset Books* and *Sunset Magazine*

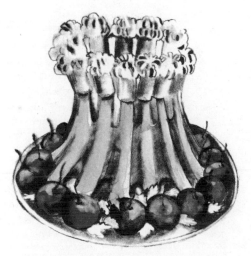

LANE BOOKS • MENLO PARK, CALIFORNIA

Foreword

There is no one way to give a perfect dinner party, and this, of course, is the reason entertaining can be so much fun. In this book we suggest ways to handle a variety of situations which any host or hostess can expect to encounter: large groups to small; formal situations to extremely casual gatherings; complex, well-planned functions to spur-of-the-moment gatherings; dinners for holidays and dinners that are simply a congenial gathering of friends; and also menus that reflect interest in cuisines of other lands. In each chapter that follows are specific directions for planning and organizing these many different kinds of dinners. The objective of each menu is to make the occasion as enjoyable for those who are giving the party as for the guests. There is considerable emphasis on steps that can, when feasible, be completed ahead, plus concrete suggestions on how to serve each meal. These menus have all been prepared in Sunset's test kitchen by the home economics staff, and have been highly rated by panels of taste testers.

Edited by Judith A. Gaulke

Special Consultant: Jerry Anne Di Vecchio
ASSOCIATE HOME ECONOMICS EDITOR,
SUNSET MAGAZINE

Illustrations: Susan S. Lampton

Design: Lawrence A. Laukhuf

Cover: Crown roast, see recipe on page 67.
Photographed by George Selland, Moss Photography.
Design Consultant: John Flack.

Photographers: Glenn M. Christiansen: pages 18, 30.
Darrow M. Watt: pages 4, 46, 60.

Executive Editor, Sunset Books: David E. Clark

Fourth Printing December 1973

Contents

Holidays Special

*O*n holidays when family or friends gather to celebrate the special occasion, dinners such as in this chapter can become the highlight of the day. Some of the menus fit traditional patterns, others provide for innovation. All incorporate suggestions for preparation steps that can be completed ahead. For the most part, these holiday meals are scaled for groups of 6 to 8, but the Thanksgiving turkey dinner and the Christmas roast beef meal will accommodate larger numbers. The menus suggest mood and scene changes, too; an intimate dinner for two on Valentines' day calls for a candlelit table, while a Halloween supper can be gaily served to guests comfortable on cushions around a glowing fireplace. You start with a New Year's Eve Party and travel through the calendar year to Christmas.

A hollowed-out pumpkin is the serving container for the creamy carrot soup which highlights this menu. A cheese pie, salad, broccoli, and bread sticks complete the holiday meal. Serve your production in front of a blazing fireplace with beverages of your choice. The menu and recipes can be found on page 12.

New Year's Eve Dinner Party

GREEN SALAD WITH PUMPKIN SEEDS

GLAZED CORNED BEEF

CRANBERRY ICE IN LEMON SHELLS

DOLLAR POTATOES

BROCCOLI SPEARS

TOFFEE RUM CAKE

A handsome corned beef roast, ringed with lemon shells holding fruit ice, is the entrée for this flexible menu that serves 8, or you can double that number with ease.

Bake or buy the plain cake then assemble and chill it early in the day. Simmer the beef in the morning, if you wish, and glaze it just before serving in the same oven with the potatoes. Cook fresh or frozen broccoli shortly before dinner. Mix your favorite green salad with an oil and vinegar dressing and sprinkle pumpkin seeds over it.

Glazed Corned Beef

3 quarts water
6 to 8-pound corned beef (round or rump)
1 bay leaf
1 small onion, quartered
1 stalk celery, cut up
2 to 3 strips orange peel pared with a vegetable peeler
    Whole cloves
2 tablespoons honey
1 tablespoon Dijon-style mustard
2 tablespoons thawed frozen orange juice concentrate
    Lemon shells (directions follow)

Bring water to a boil in a large kettle; add corned beef, bay leaf, onion, celery, orange peel. Cover and simmer about 4 hours or until meat is tender when pierced. (At this point you can chill meat in broth, reheat before using.)

Remove meat from liquid to a roasting pan with rack, placing meat fat side up. With a sharp knife, score the fat into diamonds and decorate with whole cloves. Mix together the honey, mustard, and thawed orange juice concentrate. Spoon half of it over the roast. Bake in

a 375° oven for 30 minutes, brushing several times with remaining sauce.

Place meat on a carving board and ring with lemon shells. Slice meat thinly. Makes 8 to 10 servings.

Cranberry Ice in Lemon Shells

Cut 4 or 5 large lemons in half and ream juice from them (save juice for other uses). Cut a thin slice from the base of each shell so it will stand upright. Fill with a scoop of cranberry ice or other fruit ice or sherbet (you need about 1 quart). Freeze, covered. Makes 10 servings.

Dollar Potatoes

Scrub 4 large potatoes, leaving on skins. Cut crosswise in about 3/16-inch slices keeping potato shape intact. Arrange in 2 rows, with slices upright, in a buttered 5 by 9-inch loaf pan. Melt 1/2 cup butter, add 2 green onions, finely chopped, and pour over potatoes. Bake, uncovered, in a 425° oven for 1 hour; reduce heat to 375° and bake 30 minutes longer, or until tender. Turn out of pan onto a platter to serve. Makes 8 to 10 servings.

Toffee Rum Cake

1 10-inch sponge or chiffon cake
1/2 cup sugar
3/4 cup water
1/4 cup rum or brandy or 2 tablespoons frozen orange juice concentrate, thawed
1 to 1-1/2 cups whipping cream
2 tablespoons sugar
1 teaspoon vanilla
4 ounces chocolate-covered English toffee

Place cake on a serving platter and use a wooden skewer to make holes 1 inch apart all the way through the cake. Simmer the 1/2 cup sugar and water for 5 minutes. Remove from heat and add rum, brandy, or orange juice concentrate. Pour hot syrup slowly over cake. Chill.

Whip cream with the 2 tablespoons sugar until soft peaks form; stir in vanilla. Spread over top and sides of cake. Coarsely chop English toffee; sprinkle on top of cake. Chill up to 12 hours. Makes 12 to 14 servings.

Valentine Dinner for Two

MIXED SALAD GREENS OIL AND VINEGAR
DRESSING

CRAB AND MUSHROOM RAMEKINS

BUTTERED ASPARAGUS SPEARS

CRUSTY DINNER ROLLS   BUTTER

FLAMING CHERRY SUNDAES

A candlelight dinner for two is especially appropriate for Valentine's Day. This simple yet refined menu is designed for leisurely dining with minimum last minute preparation.

You can prepare the individual casseroles early in the day and heat them in the oven while you enjoy the salad. Use either fresh or frozen asparagus spears and packaged dinner rolls. For a festive finale, warm and flame the cherry sauce (made in advance) at the table in a small chafing dish or pan over a denatured alcohol burner.

Crab and Mushroom Ramekins

   2   tablespoons butter or margarine
 1/2   pound mushrooms, sliced
1-1/2 tablespoons all-purpose flour
 2/3   cup dry white wine
 1/2   cup sour cream
 3/4   cup shredded Swiss cheese
 3/4   pound crab
       Salt and pepper
       Toasted slivered almonds (optional)

In a frying pan over medium heat, melt the butter and sauté the mushrooms until golden brown. Lift out a few mushrooms and set aside for garnish. Sprinkle remaining mushrooms with flour and stir until bubbly. Remove from heat and slowly add the white wine. Return to heat and cook, stirring, until thickened. Stir in sour cream, cheese, and crab. Season to taste with salt and pepper.

Spoon mixture into two individual-serving size shallow baking dishes and garnish with reserved mushrooms and slivered almonds, if you wish. (Cover and refrigerate

if made ahead.) Heat, uncovered, in a 325° oven for 10 to 15 minutes (20 to 30 minutes if refrigerated). Makes 2 servings.

Flaming Cherry Sundaes

   1   can (about 1 lb.) pitted dark sweet cherries
   1   tablespoon cornstarch
   2   tablespoons sugar
       Dash each salt and cinnamon
   1   tablespoon lemon juice
 1/4   cup warmed brandy
       Vanilla ice cream

Drain cherries, saving 1/2 cup of the syrup. In a saucepan combine cornstarch, reserved syrup, sugar, salt, and cinnamon. Bring to a boil, stirring, and cook until liquid is clear and thickened. Remove from heat and stir in lemon juice and cherries. Cover and set aside until needed. Heat just before serving; pour brandy over fruit and ignite. Spoon flaming fruit and sauce over individual servings of ice cream. Makes 2 servings.

Seafood Supper for Mother's Day

AVOCADO ALMOND SALAD

DANISH SOLE AND SHRIMP OVEN ENTREE

BUTTERED GREEN BEANS

CHEESECAKE WITH CHERRY JAM

Most of the preparation for the delicately seasoned entrée can be done a day ahead in case Mother is her own hostess for the "special" day. You assemble and bake the casserole just before dinner. The salad can be served before or with the fish. Buy a cheesecake (or bake your own) and top cool wedges with cherry jam.

Avocado Almond Salad

6   cups bite-sized pieces butter lettuce
1   avocado, peeled and sliced
4   tablespoons prepared roasted, diced almonds
3   tablespoons red wine vinegar
6   tablespoons olive oil
1/2   teaspoon salt

Place lettuce in a salad bowl. Arrange the avocado on the lettuce and sprinkle with the almonds. Mix wine vinegar with the olive oil and salt; pour over greens and mix. Makes 6 servings.

Danish Sole and Shrimp Oven Entrée

2   pounds small sole fillets
    Salt and pepper to taste
3   tablespoons each lemon juice and butter
    About 1 cup half-and-half or milk
3   tablespoons each all-purpose flour and shredded Parmesan cheese
1/2   pound small, cooked, shelled, and deveined shrimp
1   package (8 oz.) frozen potato puffs

Fold each piece of sole in half and arrange side by side in a shallow casserole (8 by 10 inches or 1-1/2 to 2-quart size). Sprinkle fish lightly with salt, pepper, and lemon juice; dot with 1 tablespoon of the butter. Cover and bake in a 425° oven for 20 minutes.

Remove casserole from oven and let stand until slightly cooled. Holding fish in place with a lid or wide spatula, drain juices from casserole into a measuring cup. Add half-and-half to make 1-3/4 cups total liquid.

Melt remaining 2 tablespoons butter in a saucepan, blend in flour, and then gradually add the juices and cream, blending smoothly. Cook, stirring, until boiling. Blend in 2 tablespoons of the cheese. At this point both the fish and the sauce, each covered, can be chilled overnight.

Distribute all but a few of the shrimp over the sole. Spoon sauce, hot or cold (stir to soften), evenly over the fish; edge casserole with frozen potato puffs. Sprinkle sauce with remaining 1 tablespoon cheese. Bake uncovered in a 475° oven until bubbling; allow 20 minutes for the chilled casserole, or 10 minutes for the casserole with hot sauce. Garnish with the reserved shrimp. Makes 6 servings.

Buttered Green Beans

If you serve fresh whole green beans, try cooking them as much as a day ahead, uncovered, in a quantity of boiling salted water just until tender. Then drain beans, immerse in ice water to chill, drain again, wrap and refrigerate. At serving time immerse beans in hot water just until warmed through and then drain; they keep their color better and require little attention. Allow 1-1/2 pounds for 6 servings.

When the Relatives Arrive for Easter

ORANGE AND SWEET ONION SALAD

HOT VEGETABLE PLATTER WITH
PARSLEY BUTTER

BAKED HAM WITH MADEIRA SAUCE

STRAWBERRY SHORTCAKES

Baked ham is the mainstay of this menu, offering flexibility for an unpredictable number of guests. The accompaniments make few demands on the cook.

Orange and Sweet Onion Salad

4   large oranges
1   medium-sized mild onion
1/3   cup pitted ripe olives
2   tablespoons white wine vinegar
1/3   cup olive oil
1/2   teaspoon each salt and tarragon

Several hours in advance, cut the peel and white membrane from oranges and slice fruit thinly; place in a shallow salad bowl and chill, covered. About 1 hour before serving, peel and thinly slice sweet onion; separate into rings and tuck between orange slices. Scatter olives on top. Mix together white wine vinegar, olive oil, salt, and tarragon; pour over salad. Cover and chill until serving time. Makes 8 servings.

Hot Vegetable Platter

1-1/2   pounds asparagus
        About 2 cups cherry tomatoes
12   small new potatoes
        Boiling salted water
3   tablespoons butter
1   teaspoon sugar
1/2   teaspoon salt
        Parsley butter (recipe follows)

Early in the day, wash and trim ends from asparagus and wash and remove stems from cherry tomatoes; package in plastic bags and store in the refrigerator.

Shortly before serving, wash potatoes and cook in boiling salted water to cover until tender; drain. Cook asparagus in a wide shallow uncovered pan of boiling salted water until tender; drain and dress with 1 tablespoon of the butter. Also, sauté cherry tomatoes in the remaining 2 tablespoons butter along with sugar and salt, over high heat, shaking pan and heating just until hot through, about 2 minutes.

Arrange potatoes, asparagus, and tomatoes on a large hot platter. Serve with parsley butter to spoon onto individual portions. Makes 8 servings.

Parsley Butter:

Cream 3/4 cup (3/8 lb.) soft butter or margarine and blend in 1/2 teaspoon grated lemon peel and 2 tablespoons minced parsley. Chill; serve at room temperature.

Baked Ham with Madeira Sauce

    7-pound section of ham with bone; either half-butt or shank end
2   tablespoon Dijon-style mustard
1/2   cup brown sugar, firmly packed
1/2   cup Madeira wine

Place ham on a rack in a roasting pan and insert a meat thermometer into the thickest part. Roast in a 300° oven until meat thermometer registers 160° (allow about 2-1/2 hours or 22 minutes to the pound). Remove from oven and, with a sharp pointed knife, score the top fat in a diamond design.

Mix together mustard, brown sugar, and Madeira; spoon half of it over ham. Put meat back into oven reset to 375°, and roast until ham is glazed a golden brown, about 15 minutes longer; baste occasionally with remaining Madeira sauce. Serve hot (leftovers are good cold). Makes about 14 to 16 servings.

Strawberry Shortcakes

Open 1 package (about 8-1/2 oz.) refrigerated butter-flake dinner rolls and separate into layers. Using 6 rounds for each shortcake, arrange them on an ungreased baking sheet in a flower design with 1 round in the center and 5 around the edge; press together to seal. You should have 8 shortcakes. Bake in a 375° oven for about 12 minutes, or until golden brown. Remove pan from oven, brush Shortcakes with 2 tablespoons apricot jam, and continue baking about 3 minutes longer, or until glazed. Place pan on rack to cool.

At serving time, top equally with 1 cup heavy cream, whipped and sweetened to taste, and 2 cups halved strawberries. Makes 8 servings.

Memorial Day Dinner

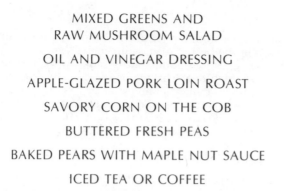

MIXED GREENS AND
RAW MUSHROOM SALAD

OIL AND VINEGAR DRESSING

APPLE-GLAZED PORK LOIN ROAST

SAVORY CORN ON THE COB

BUTTERED FRESH PEAS

BAKED PEARS WITH MAPLE NUT SAUCE

ICED TEA OR COFFEE

This dinner allows you a choice of oven-roasting the pork loin and corn or cooking them in a covered barbecue. The meat can roast untended for an hour or so, but should be basted frequently during the remaining 1 to 1-1/2 hours of cooking. The foil-wrapped corn cooks along with the pork roast during the last half hour.

A pork loin roast is easy to carve if you ask your meatman to saw through the back bone between each rib and then tie the roast together. To serve, cut the cord from the roast and slice meat apart into chops.

The rest of the meal goes together quickly and is easy to transport to the garden.

For the salad, combine romaine with butter lettuce or red leaf lettuce, and watercress, top with a few sliced fresh mushrooms, and use a prepared oil and vinegar dressing.

Apple-Glazed Pork Loin Roast

3-1/2 to 4-pound pork loin roast
   1 cup apple juice
   3 tablespoons soy sauce
   1 clove garlic, minced or mashed
 1/4 teaspoon ground ginger
1-1/2 teaspoons each cornstarch and water

To oven-roast the pork, place meat, fat side up, on a rack in a shallow baking pan. Roast, uncovered, in a 325° oven for 1 hour.

To roast the pork on a covered barbecue, spread medium-low well ignited coals in a ring around a drip pan in the center of the fire grate. Place meat, fat side up, on the grill about 6 inches above the pan. Cover barbecue, open the temperature control dampers, and cook meat for about 1 hour.

Meanwhile, combine the apple juice, soy sauce, garlic, and ginger.

After 1 hour of cooking, baste roast generously with the apple juice mixture. Continue to cook the pork for 1 to 1-1/2 hours more or until meat thermometer inserted in the center (not touching bone) registers 170°, basting every 15 minutes with the remaining apple juice mixture. (After the first hour you will need to add more charcoal to barbecue to maintain heat level.) Remove meat to a warm platter. To make gravy, skim fat from the pan drippings; combine the cornstarch and water, stir into the drippings, and cook, stirring, until thickened. Serve the gravy in a bowl to spoon over pork. Makes 6 servings.

Savory Corn on the Cob

   3 tablespoons mayonnaise
   1 large clove garlic, minced or mashed
   1 teaspoon olive oil
 1/2 teaspoon smoke-flavored salt
     Dash pepper
   6 ears corn

In a small bowl, combine mayonnaise, garlic, olive oil, salt, and pepper. Husk corn; spread ears evenly with mayonnaise mixture and wrap each ear tightly in foil. Roast in a 325° oven (or in a covered barbecue over low coals) for about 30 minutes, or until tender. Remove foil from corn and serve at once. Makes 6 servings.

Baked Pears with Maple Nut Sauce

   3 medium-sized, firm ripe pears, cut in half lengthwise and cored
 1/2 cup each water, maple-flavored syrup, and dark brown sugar, firmly packed
   1 teaspoon maple flavoring
   2 tablespoons melted butter
 1/4 cup chopped pecans

Place pear halves, cut side up, close together in a small, deep casserole. Combine water, syrup, sugar, maple flavoring, and butter; pour over pears. Cover and bake in a 400° oven until pears are tender (about 40 minutes). While still slightly warm, serve in individual sauce dishes with some of the syrup. Sprinkle each serving with nuts. Makes 6 servings.

4th of July Barbecue

BROWN AND WHITE RICE CASSEROLE

BARBECUED BEEF STEAK

HOT BUTTERED ITALIAN GREEN BEANS

TOMATO AND SWEET ONION PLATTER

SOUR DOUGH FRENCH BREAD

FRESH BERRY SUNDAES

This festive meal centers on a thick steak big enough to serve about six people; it's a fine choice for entertaining. While the steak is cooking, the rice casserole bakes in the oven, and the salad platter mellows in the refrigerator.

Much of this dinner can be prepared ahead. Early in the day, assemble the rice casserole; let stand at room temperature until time to bake, adding the boiling broth just before you tuck it in the oven. Also prepare the salad platter several hours in advance; cover and chill until needed. Wash and snip the ends from the beans; cook 3 to 4 minutes or until tender in an uncovered pan of rapidly boiling water just before serving.

Brown and White Rice Casserole

    6   slices chopped bacon
    4   green onions including some of the green tops, sliced
  1/2   pound mushrooms, sliced
    6   tablespoons butter
  1/4   cup slivered almonds
  3/4   cup each quick-cooking brown rice and long or short grain white rice
  1/4   teaspoon each salt, pepper, thyme, and marjoram
3-1/4   cups boiling regular-strength beef broth
    2   tablespoons Parmesan cheese, shredded

In a frying pan, cook chopped bacon slices until crisp. With a slotted spoon, lift bacon from pan into a 2-1/2-quart casserole. Discard bacon drippings. In the same pan, sauté the green onions and mushrooms in 2 tablespoons of the butter; cook until limp and lightly browned. Turn into casserole. In the same frying pan, toast the slivered almonds and rice until golden brown in 3 more tablespoons butter, stirring. Turn rice mixture into casserole and season with salt, pepper, thyme, and marjoram. This much can be done ahead and held at room temperature.

Just before baking, pour in beef broth, stir well, cover,

and bake in a 350° oven for 40 minutes. Uncover, stir, dot with 1 tablespoon butter, and sprinkle with Parmesan cheese. Cover and bake 10 minutes longer. Makes 6 servings.

Barbecued Beef Steak

This should be a large steak that when cut about 2 inches thick will weigh about 3 to 3-1/2 pounds. You can use a porterhouse, top sirloin, or first cut of the top round. If you buy a less tender cut, use a commercial meat tenderizer as directed on the package.

Barbecue the steak over medium-hot coals 6 inches from heat, turning about every 10 minutes. It will take about 30 to 45 minutes for rare steak. For best results, insert a meat thermometer in the center of the steak and cook to 130° for rare, or 140° for medium-rare. To serve, place steak on a serving platter, season with salt and pepper, and cut across the grain into thin slices. Makes 6 servings.

Tomato and Sweet Onion Platter

    3   large tomatoes
    1   large mild onion, thinly sliced
    1   large cucumber, peeled and thinly sliced
    1   large green pepper, seeded and cut into rings
  1/2   teaspoon salt
  1/4   teaspoon pepper
  1/2   teaspoon salad herbs or crumbled basil
  1/4   cup salad oil
    2   tablespoons white wine vinegar

Peel and cut tomatoes into 1/4-inch-thick slices; arrange in a single layer on a large rimmed platter. Separate onion slices into rings and arrange over tomatoes; top with the cucumber slices and then distribute pepper rings over all. Sprinkle with salt, pepper, and salad herbs. Drizzle salad oil and vinegar evenly over all. Cover and refrigerate as long as 4 hours. To serve, spoon some of the dressing over each portion. Makes 6 servings.

Fresh Berry Sundaes

Sweeten to taste fresh berries of your choice; slice strawberries, blueberries, or raspberries. Allow 1/2 to 3/4 cup fruit for each serving. Serve at room temperature to preserve their natural flavor. Ladle over scoops of vanilla ice cream for a light dessert.

Halloween Guest Dinner

CARROT SOUP

GREEN SALAD

SAVORY CHEESE PIE

BUTTERED BROCCOLI

BREAD STICKS

SPICY ORANGE SUNDAES

Stage this informal dinner for six in the living room, preferably near a fireplace. It's fun to serve on a large, low table with your guests sitting around the floor on large cushions. A pumpkin shell may be used as a container for the carrot soup. To serve soup, warm shell first by filling with boiling water, then drain. (You can make the soup the night before—but the pumpkin is best if seeds are removed no more than 5 hours before you plan to use it.)

Put the cheese pie in the oven about 30 minutes before you plan to start the meal. Cook broccoli and heat soup just before serving. The dessert can be made on the morning of the party.

Carrot Soup

    4   to 6 large carrots, sliced (about 2-1/2 cups)
  1/2   teaspoon salt
1-3/4   cups water
    1   can (13 oz.) undiluted evaporated milk
  1/4   teaspoon each coarse ground pepper and nutmeg
    1   tablespoon minced parsley

Cook carrots in the boiling salted water until tender. Put carrots and liquid, a portion at a time, in a blender jar and whirl, covered, until smooth. Return to saucepan and stir in evaporated milk, pepper, nutmeg, and parsley. (Refrigerate if made ahead.) Bring to a boil, and serve. Makes 6 to 8 servings.

Green Salad

1   small head each iceberg lettuce and romaine
    About 1/2 cup prepared Italian style dressing

Tear lettuce and romaine into small pieces. Mix with dressing just before serving. (In the spirit of the occasion, you might serve the salad in an iron pot resembling a witch's caldron.) Makes 6 to 8 servings.

Savory Cheese Pie

  1/2   teaspoon black pepper
  1/4   teaspoon each dry mustard and paprika
        Pastry mix for a double-crust 9-inch pie
  1/2   pound sharp Cheddar cheese, shredded (about 2-1/2 cups)
    2   eggs
  2/3   cup milk
  1/4   teaspoon salt
1-1/2   tablespoons finely chopped onion
    2   medium-sized tomatoes, peeled and sliced
        Beaten egg

Work pepper, mustard, and paprika into the pastry as you blend it according to package directions. Divide pastry into 2 equal portions. Roll one section out on a floured board and use it to line a 9-inch pie pan. Distribute shredded cheese in pan. Beat the 2 eggs with milk, salt, and onion; pour over cheese. Cover with a layer of tomato slices. Roll remaining pastry out on floured board and cover filling. Seal, slash top, and crimp rim decoratively: Reserve scraps, reroll and make 2 or 3 pastry shaped leaves and place on center of pie. Brush top with beaten egg. Bake at 425° for 10 minutes, reduce heat to 325° and cook 30 minutes longer or until well browned. Serve hot. Makes 6 servings.

Spicy Orange Sundae

    3   medium-sized oranges
  3/4   cup sugar
    1   teaspoon cornstarch
  3/4   teaspoon ground ginger
  1/2   teaspoon ground cinnamon
    2   tablespoons raisins
        About 1-1/2 pints vanilla ice cream

Halve oranges, making zigzag edges. Cut out orange pulp using a grapefruit knife. Scrape free and remove any remaining pulp with a spoon; rinse shells, dry, and put them in the freezer. Meanwhile, remove seeds and fibrous material from the orange. Put the orange pieces in a saucepan with a mixture of sugar, cornstarch, ginger, cinnamon, and raisins; bring to a boil, stirring, and cook until thickened slightly. Chill, covered.

Remove orange shells from freezer and fill each with a scoop of vanilla ice cream. Cover with foil or plastic wrap and return to freezer until serving time. To serve, put each filled orange shell in a small dish and pass the spicy orange syrup in a pitcher to pour over ice cream. Makes 6 sundaes.

Traditional Thanksgiving

This is a traditional menu in many ways and is designed to be served as a leisurely five-course meal—appetizers, soup, turkey with accompaniments, salad with cheese, dessert and coffee.

Prepare the turkey and stuffing the night before and chill separately—but do not stuff until just before roasting. Make prune and bacon garnish ahead and chill; bake it while the turkey is "resting" out of the oven for 20 to 30 minutes before carving. Dice assorted cheeses such as Swiss, Fontinella, Gruyére, or Port Salut, just before dinner to let them reach full flavor at room temperature: Toss with bite-sized pieces of Romaine and a prepared oil and vinegar dressing. Allow 2 tablespoons cheese, 3/4 to 1 cup greens and 1 to 2 tablespoons dressing for each serving.

Caviar - Oyster Canapés

10   slices white bread
1   jar (3-1/2 oz.) caviar
20   smoked oysters
     Lemon juice

Toast bread slices lightly on both sides and then cut 20 circles 1-1/2 inch diameter. Spread evenly with caviar and top each circle with a smoked oyster. Sprinkle lightly with lemon juice. Makes 20 appetizers.

Consommé with Sherry

Flavor each 10-1/2-ounce can condensed consommé with 1 tablespoon Sherry. Serve hot in cups; allow 3/4 to 1 cup for each serving.

Roast Turkey, Almond Stuffing

Thaw turkey if frozen; rinse bird inside and out; pat dry.

2   cups minced onion
1-3/4   cups melted butter
2   cups celery, thinly sliced
2   teaspoons salt
1   teaspoon each thyme, marjoram, savory, and sage
10   cups toasted stale bread crumbs
2-1/2   cups slivered toasted almonds
     Hot water
     16-pound turkey

Cook onion in 1-1/2 cups of the butter until golden. Combine with celery, salt, thyme, marjoram, savory, sage, bread, and almonds. Squeeze some dressing together tightly in your hand; if it won't stay together when released, add a little hot water. Fill body and breast cavities with stuffing and skewer shut. Place turkey, breast up, on a rack in a pan. Leave legs free and tuck wing tips under bird. Brush with some of the remaining 1/4 cup butter.

Bake in a 325° oven for about 3-3/4 hours or until a thermometer in thickest part of breast registers 175°. Brush occasionally with butter. Let turkey stand 20 to 30 minutes at room temperature before carving. Makes 12 to 16 servings.

Prune and Bacon Garnish

Insert a stuffed green olive into a pitted prune. Wrap each with half a slice of bacon, and bake in a 350° oven until bacon is crisp, about 20 minutes. Allow 2 to 3 for a serving.

Ice Cream with Mincemeat Sauce

Top each serving of vanilla ice cream with a dollop of hot prepared mincemeat. Serve at once. For a more spectacular dessert, heat mincemeat at the table in a chafing dish; light 1/4 cup warm brandy (for each pint of mincemeat) and pour into mincemeat. Spoon sauce over the ice cream while it's still burning.

An Elegant Thanksgiving

OPEN-FACED APPETIZER SANDWICHES

CHAMPAGNE

ROAST GOOSE WITH NEW POTATOES

GLAZED APPLE SLICES AND PRUNES

BUTTERED BROCCOLI SPEARS

MIXED GREEN SALAD

PORT SALUT CHEESE

ICE CREAM TOWER WITH FLAMING RUM

SAUCE

This elegant Thanksgiving dinner serves 6 and is very easy to handle. The roast goose adds new dimension to tradition.

Start by freezing the ice cream mold the day before. As guests arrive, ready and waiting are appetizer sandwiches and champagne. Thanksgiving morning, assemble the sandwiches, arrange on a serving tray, cover with clear plastic film, and chill until guests arrive. For each person allow 2 or 3 thin slices of small buffet-style rye or long slender French bread. Spread some of the slices with sweet butter and top with radish slices; spread other slices with soft cream cheese (plain or with chives) and mound on each 1 to 2 tablespoons small whole cooked shrimp, garnishing with watercress leaves or parsley sprigs; also spoon chunks of prepared herring in sour cream on buttered bread, bordering fish with minced green onion.

Crisp the greens for the salad; you will need about 6 to 8 cups broken pieces. Choose a varied combination such as part curly endive, butter lettuce, and watercress; wash, drain well, and wrap greens in a towel; enclose in a plastic bag and chill. To serve, mix with about 1/2 cup of your favorite oil and vinegar dressing or a purchased one. Spoon salad onto individual plates. Pass sliced Port Salut cheese and invite each person to cut the portion he desires from a 3/4 pound piece.

Calculate timing so goose and potatoes will be done about 1/2 hour before you want to serve them; the fruit and broccoli can cook while the goose rests for carving, then are used to adorn the platter.

Roast Goose with New Potatoes

9 to 10-pound goose, thawed if frozen
   Salt and pepper
3 or 4 medium-sized onions, quartered (optional)
12 to 15 small, whole, unpeeled new potatoes
   Glazed apple slices and prunes (recipe follows)

Rinse goose well with cold water, remove any large layers of fat from the cavities, and wipe dry. Sprinkle inside with salt and pepper; stuff with onion quarters, if desired. To close the wishbone cavity, bring neck skin over back and fasten with a skewer. Turn bird over and skewer body cavity closed. Tie drumsticks together. Place the goose, breast side down, on a rack in a deep pan, or use heavy foil to build up higher sides on a shallow roasting pan (it helps prevent oven splatter).

Roast, uncovered, in a 325° oven for 3-1/2 to 4 hours, or until drumstick meat feels soft. Spoon or siphon off fat as it accumulates in the pan. The last 1-1/2 hours turn bird and roast breast side up.

One hour before the goose is done, add the new potatoes to the pan drippings. Baste and turn occasionally until tender and lightly browned.

To serve, lift goose from roasting pan, remove skewers and string, and place breast side up on the serving platter. Use a slotted spoon to lift out the potatoes; pile beside the bird. Cover with foil and keep warm. Serve on a large platter (choose one about 15 to 20 inches long). Surround with glazed apples and prunes and broccoli. Makes 6 servings.

Glazed Apple Slices and Prunes

1/2 pound moist-packed, pitted prunes
   Water
1/4 cup butter
3 large apples (Golden Delicious or Winesap), peeled, cored, and thickly sliced
1 tablespoon firmly packed brown sugar
1/2 teaspoon cinnamon

Plump prunes in hot water to cover for 10 minutes. Drain. Melt butter in a wide frying pan, add apples, and cook over moderately high heat, turning gently with a wide spatula until fruit begins to soften and looks translucent, about 8 minutes. Sprinkle with brown sugar and cinnamon and cook, turning, until evenly glazed. Lift apple slices to the large serving platter (with the goose); add prunes to pan and turn over in remaining syrup for 2 to 3 minutes to heat through. Arrange prunes among the apple slices.

Buttered Broccoli Spears

Trim and wash 1-1/2 pounds broccoli. In a wide shallow pan bring to boiling about 1-1/2 inches salted water. Add broccoli and cook, uncovered, until just tender, about 10 to 12 minutes. Drain; season with salt, pepper, and butter to taste. Arrange on platter with goose.

Ice Cream Tower with Flaming Rum Sauce

1-1/2 to 2 quarts toasted almond or pumpkin flavor ice cream

1/2 cup each *butter, water,* and *firmly packed brown sugar*

3 tablespoons *warm rum*

In a tall 1-1/2-quart fancy mold, firmly pack ice cream. Cover and freeze overnight or up to several weeks.

At least 6 to 8 hours before serving, immerse mold in hottest tap water for 5 to 10 seconds, then unmold ice cream on a cold serving dish; immediately return to freezer. When firm, cover the ice cream with clear plastic film.

To make rum sauce, bring to a boil, stirring, the butter, water, and brown sugar; cook until sugar dissolves.

At serving time, place sauce in a fondue pan or chafing dish over direct heat and warm. Ignite warm rum and pour at once into sauce, stirring. Carve ice cream into bowls and ladle hot sauce over it. Makes 1 cup sauce. Serves 6.

Christmas Dinner Featuring Roast Beef

CLAMS (OR OYSTERS) CASINO

MINIATURE BROWN BREAD AND BUTTER SANDWICHES

RIB ROAST OF BEEF   HORSERADISH SAUCE

HERBED YORKSHIRE PUDDING

SPINACH WITH MUSHROOMS

ROMAINE SALAD

CAMEMBERT CHEESE   TOASTED CRACKERS

STEAMED FRUIT PUDDING   HARD SAUCE

Roast beef dinner is a Christmas tradition for many people. In this menu, the roast follows a first course of Clams or Oysters Casino. You can make the Yorkshire pudding and cook the spinach after the beef comes out of the oven—let the roast "rest," covered, for easy carving. Serve the salad as a separate course, accompanied by Camembert cheese and toasted crackers. Make the dressing ahead, but tear the crisp greens and toss the salad just before serving. Flaming plum pudding tops off the meal.

Clams or Oysters Casino

Allow 6 clams or oysters in the shell for each serving. Have an ovenproof plate for each serving and half fill it with ice cream salt. Heat salt filled dishes in a 400° oven for 15 minutes. Open clams or oysters (or have it done at the market) and discard top shells. Leave meat and juices in bottom shells and arrange them on salt so they are level.

Sprinkle each mollusk with about 1 teaspoon of the chopped green and red pepper blended in equal parts (use canned pimiento if you can't find red pepper) and top with 1 inch segments of thin sliced bacon. Return the dishes to the 400° oven until the bacon is crisp. Serve in the salt lined dishes with wedges of lemon and brown bread-and-butter sandwiches.

Rib Roast of Beef

Select a large roast, preferably 5 or 6 ribs (about 10–12 lbs.), allowing 1 pound for each person. Have chine bone cut and ribs cut short. Sprinkle with salt and place, fat side up, on a rack in a pan. Roast in a 325° oven and cook until the meat thermometer reaches 120°–130° for rare (18–20 minutes per lb.), 140°–150° for medium-rare (about 25 minutes per lb.). Remove from oven and cover lightly to keep warm and firm for slicing while the Yorkshire pudding bakes. Serve the roast on a large platter.

Horseradish Sauce

1/4   cup drained prepared horseradish
1/2   teaspoon salt
  1   cup (1/2 pt.) sour cream

Combine horseradish, salt, and sour cream. Cover and chill until ready to serve; place in a small bowl. Makes 6 to 8 servings.

Herbed Yorkshire Pudding

       Beef drippings
  1   cup all-purpose flour
  3   eggs
1-1/4 cups milk
  1   teaspoon salt
  1   tablespoon minced parsley
1/4   teaspoon each rosemary and thyme

Pour 1-1/2 tablespoons of hot drippings from beef roast into each of 6 to 8 glass custard cups (6 oz. size) or 6 to 8 sections of 2 inch muffin or popover pans. Sift flour, measure. Beat eggs to blend well with milk. Stir in flour, salt, parsley, rosemary and thyme, and mix until smooth. Pour into the prepared dishes and bake for 15 minutes in a 450° oven. Reduce heat to 350° and bake another 10 to 15 minutes, or until puffy and brown. Serve at once. Makes 6 to 8 servings.

Spinach with Mushrooms

  2   pounds spinach
1/2   pound mushrooms, sliced
  4   tablespoons butter
  1   clove garlic, minced or mashed
  3   tablespoons all-purpose flour
  1   cup half-and-half
       Salt and pepper
       Pimiento

Wash spinach well, trim off and discard stems and drain leaves. Sauté mushrooms in 2 tablespoons of the butter until limp and liquid is evaporated; set aside. Heat remaining 2 tablespoons butter with garlic; stir in flour, and cook until golden, stirring. Gradually blend in cream; cook, stirring, until thickened. Set aside.

Place spinach in a covered kettle and cook over medium heat just until wilted. Drain and chop very fine. Combine with mushrooms and cream sauce and heat through. Season to taste with salt and pepper. Pour into a serving dish, and decorate with stars cut from pimiento. Makes 6 servings.

Steamed Fruit Pudding

1/3   cup butter
3/4   cup firmly packed brown sugar
  1   egg, beaten
  2   tablespoons dry red or white wine
1/2   cup each currants, chopped raisins, and chopped dates
1/3   cup each chopped candied pineapple, candied cherries, pecans, and citron
  1   cup sifted all-purpose flour
1/2   teaspoon soda
1/4   teaspoon each salt and cinnamon
1/8   teaspoon each ground allspice, ginger, and nutmeg
       Sugar

Cream butter with brown sugar; beat in egg. Add wine, currants, raisins, dates, pineapple, cherries, pecans, and citron. Mix the flour with soda, salt, cinnamon, allspice, ginger, and nutmeg and thoroughly blend with creamed mixture.

Butter a 1-quart pudding mold and dust with sugar. Pour in pudding; cover tightly. Set mold on a rack in a deep pan and cover. Maintain several inches of boiling water in pan for 4 hours. Cool; unmold. Slice to serve. Makes 6 servings.

Hard Sauce

Beat 2 cups sifted powdered sugar with 1/2 cup (1/4 lb.) soft butter until mixture is fluffy. Beat in rum or brandy to taste. Pile into serving dish. Serve at room temperature. Makes about 1-1/2 cups sauce.

Easy Christmas Chicken

BAKED CHICKEN WITH APPLE

STEAMED BROWN RICE

BUTTERED ITALIAN GREEN BEANS

LETTUCE WEDGES

THOUSAND ISLAND DRESSING

PUMPKIN CHEESE PIE

This goes together quickly. The pumpkin pie should be made ahead as it takes 1 hour to bake. If you ask another couple over, you may want to include a hot, clear broth to start the meal with. Early in the day you can brown the chicken pieces and arrange them in the casserole with the apple quarters and ginger, then cover and refrigerate. Add the liquid just before serving. While chicken is in the oven, you have time to steam the rice, cook the beans, and arrange wedges of iceberg lettuce on individual salad plates. Pass the dressing (either bottled or homemade).

Baked Chicken with Apple

    1   teaspoon salt
  1/4   teaspoon pepper
  1/8   teaspoon garlic powder
  1/2   cup flour
    3   to 3-1/2-pound broiler-fryer, cut up
    2   tablespoons each butter and salad oil
    3   firm cooking apples, peeled, cored, and quartered
    2   tablespoons sugar
    2   tablespoons finely chopped preserved or crystallized ginger
  1-1/2 cups dry white wine or apple juice
  1/2   cup water
    3   tablespoons water

In a plastic bag, combine salt, pepper, garlic powder, and flour. Shake chicken pieces in flour mixture, shake off any excess flour, and reserve extra seasoned flour. In a large frying pan, heat butter and oil over medium heat; brown chicken pieces, a few at a time, and transfer to a 2-1/2-quart casserole. Add apple quarters to pan,

sprinkle with sugar, and brown lightly. Arrange apple pieces around chicken in casserole; sprinkle with ginger. This much may be done ahead; cover and refrigerate.

Just before baking, add wine or apple juice and the 1/2 cup water to casserole. Cover and bake in a 350° oven for about 1 hour or until chicken is tender. (If not refrigerated, bake about 45 minutes.) Using a slotted spoon, remove chicken and apple to warm serving dish; keep warm. Blend reserved flour mixture with the 3 tablespoons water into a smooth paste.

Pour casserole liquid into a saucepan, stir in flour paste, and cook over medium heat stirring, until sauce is bubbly and thickened, about 5 minutes. Strain sauce to remove bits of ginger, if you wish. Spoon some of the sauce over chicken before serving. Pass remaining sauce to spoon over chicken and rice. Makes 4 servings.

Pumpkin Cheese Pie

  1-1/2 cups creamed cottage cheese
    1   tablespoon frozen orange juice concentrate, undiluted
  1-1/2 cups canned pumpkin
    3   eggs
  3/4   cup sugar
    1   teaspoon cinnamon
  1/2   teaspoon each ground ginger and allspice
  1/4   teaspoon ground cloves
        9-inch unbaked pie shell
        Whipped cream or vanilla ice cream

Combine the cottage cheese and orange juice in a blender container and blend until smooth. Add the pumpkin, eggs, sugar, cinnamon, ginger, allspice, and cloves; whirl together in the blender for about 2 minutes.

Prepare the pie shell from your own recipe or a pie crust mix; make a fluted edge. Turn pie filling into the pastry shell and bake in a 350° oven until a knife inserted in the center comes out clean, about 1 hour.

Remove pie from oven, and cool; serve at room temperature, or chill several hours before serving. If you wish, garnish with sweetened whipped cream or vanilla ice cream. Makes 6 to 8 servings.

Large Groups

When you go beyond the number of guests that can be comfortably seated at the average dinner table, then you have a crowd. And this means special menu planning. In this chapter are meals that will serve 10 to 18. For the most part they are exceptionally simple, relying heavily on main dish and side dish casseroles, salads, and large scale desserts that are assembled in part or totally in advance.

Some of the menus suggest a first course of soup or an appetizer that can be served in another room, or out-of-doors if the weather is inviting. The other menus commence with the main course.

You have several serving possibilities with these meals. You can set up small tables, presenting the foods from a buffet or a side board; perhaps you might like to change locations when serving desserts, such as moving on to the living room. Or you could serve on a large, improvised table, offering the dishes family style; another choice is to provide trays and let guests find comfortable spots in or around the house to enjoy their dinner. Use conveniences such as chafing dishes and electric warming trays to keep hot foods hot, and to maintain an unrushed atmosphere for dining.

Serving many guests can be made easy with the use of more than one room in the house. Keep main dishes hot on warming trays in the dining room while your guests enjoy appetizers or soup in the living room.

Late Evening Dinner for 12

PANCAKES POLPETTE

ASPARAGUS SPEARS, NIPPY SAUCE

CRISP RELISHES: CAULIFLOWERETTES, CARROT CURLS, STUFFED OLIVES

GLAZED APPLE BARS

These tender pancakes (actually thin crêpes) are rolled around a ground meat and spinach filling and can be assembled a day in advance.

Pancakes Polpette

2　pounds lean ground beef
1　pound bulk pork sausage
2　medium-sized onions, finely chopped
3　cloves garlic, minced or mashed
4　packages (10 oz. each) frozen chopped spinach, cooked and well drained
　　Salt to taste

Pancakes:

6　eggs
3/4　teaspoon salt
3　cups milk
2　cups regular all-purpose flour
　　Butter or margarine

Sauce:

6　cans (8 oz. each) tomato sauce
2　cups shredded sharp Cheddar cheese

Brown meats with onions and garlic, stirring. Add spinach, salt to taste, and mix well and set aside.

To make crêpes, beat eggs to blend with the 3/4 teaspoon salt and stir in milk. Sift flour, measure, and beat into egg mixture until as smooth as possible. Place 7-inch crêpe pan (or flat bottom frying pan) over medium heat and swirl enough butter in it to coat bottom. Pour in 1 tablespoon batter, tilting pan to cover the entire surface. When golden brown underneath and dry to touch on top, turn out of pan, laying flat on a clean tea towel. Continue until all batter is used, adding more butter to the pan each time. Makes approximately 36 pancakes.

Spoon an equal amount of meat filling down the center of each pancake on the cooked side, roll up, and place in a shallow baking dish seam side down. (At this point you can cover and chill overnight.) Pour tomato sauce evenly over crêpes and sprinkle with shredded cheese. Bake in a 350° oven for 30 minutes; if refrigerated, bake 40 to 45 minutes. Makes 12 servings.

Asparagus with Nippy Sauce

Trim tough ends from 6 pounds asparagus (or use 6 packages frozen asparagus spears). Cook fresh asparagus in boiling salted water to cover in a wide shallow pan, uncovered, (you may need 2 pans) just until tender; drain. Arrange on a shallow rimmed platter, and spoon over cold Nippy Sauce. To prepare sauce, mix together 1 cup prepared salad dressing (not mayonnaise), 2 tablespoons prepared mustard, and 2 tablespoons lemon juice. Makes 12 servings.

Glazed Apple Bars

12　medium-sized cooking apples
1-1/2　cups coarsely chopped walnuts
2　cups granulated sugar
2　teaspoons cinnamon
1/8　teaspoon nutmeg
2　teaspoons lemon juice
　　Pastry for 2 double crust 8 or 9-inch pies
4　tablespoons butter
3　tablespoons lemon juice
1-1/2　cups powdered sugar

Peel and slice apples; add 3/4 cup of the coarsely chopped walnuts, the granulated sugar, cinnamon, nutmeg, and the 2 teaspoons lemon juice. Stir lightly until well mixed.

Roll out half of the pastry on a floured cloth and line the bottom and sides of a 10 by 15-inch jelly roll pan. Spread apple mixture over pastry and dot with butter. Roll out the rest of the pastry on floured cloth to cover apple mixture; pinch edges to seal; prick top. Bake in a 350° oven for 1 hour.

Mix together the 3 tablespoons lemon juice and the powdered sugar; spread over hot bars, add remaining nuts. Cool, cut into bars. Makes 18 bars.

Big Ideas for a Casual Dinner

GREENS WITH AVOCADO DRESSING

CHICKEN AND MUSHROOM CASSEROLE

NOODLES ROMANOFF FRENCH BREAD

CHERRY TORTE

This dinner may be almost completely prepared an entire day in advance. Wash the salad greens and put in plastic bags in the refrigerator to crisp; also make avocado dressing. Assemble the chicken casserole and the noodles and refrigerate. Bake the dessert ahead. Before the party you need only bake the casserole and the noodles and toss the salad.

Greens with Avocado Dressing

    3   medium-sized heads romaine or 2 large heads
        iceberg lettuce
    2   fully ripe avocados
  1/2   cup lemon juice
    2   jars (6 oz. each) marinated artichoke hearts
  1/2   cup each orange juice and mayonnaise
    2   tablespoons finely chopped green onions
    1   bunch radishes, sliced
    1   cucumber, peeled and sliced

Cut out core of iceberg lettuce and hold head under lukewarm running water, gently separating the leaves just enough to clean them well. Or separate the leaves of romaine and wash well. Drain and refrigerate wrapped in paper towels or clean dish towels in the crisper unit.

In the large bowl of an electric mixer, beat avocados and lemon juice until smooth. (Or mash together with a fork.) Drain artichoke hearts and pour marinade into the avocado mixture, reserving the hearts. Add the orange juice, mayonnaise, and onions; beat until blended. Cover and refrigerate at least 4 hours or overnight.

Break the lettuce into bite-sized pieces. Cut each artichoke heart into 3 or 4 pieces. Store artichokes, radishes, and cucumber separately in the refrigerator.

At serving time, combine the lettuce, radishes, cucumber, and artichoke hearts. Pour the dressing over the vegetables and mix well. Makes about 18 servings.

Chicken and Mushroom Casserole

     36   chicken separated thighs and drumsticks (or all
          thighs)
          Salt, pepper, and paprika
    3/4   cup butter or margarine
    3/4   pound mushrooms, sliced
      4   tablespoons (1/4 cup) all-purpose flour
  1-1/2   cups regular strength chicken broth
      6   tablespoons Sherry
      3   sprigs fresh rosemary or 1/2 teaspoon crumbled dried
          rosemary

Sprinkle chicken pieces with salt, pepper, and paprika. In a wide frying pan over medium-high heat brown chicken in half the butter 15 minutes; transfer to a shallow baking pan, arranging meat in a single layer. Add remaining butter to frying pan and sauté sliced mushrooms until limp and lightly brown and liquid evaporates. Sprinkle flour over mushrooms and stir in chicken broth, Sherry, and rosemary. Cook, stirring, until thickened, then pour over chicken. (At this point you can cover and chill casserole.) Cover and bake in a 350° oven for 1 hour (if refrigerated, 1 hour 20 minutes). Makes 18 servings.

Noodles Romanoff

    2   packages (8 oz. each) egg noodles
    3   cups large curd cottage cheese
    2   cloves garlic, minced or mashed
    2   teaspoons Worcestershire
    2   cups (1 pt.) sour cream
    6   to 8 green onions, finely chopped
  1/2   teaspoon liquid hot pepper seasoning
    1   cup grated or shredded Parmesan cheese

Cook noodles according to package directions; drain well. Combine cooked noodles, cottage cheese, garlic, Worcestershire, sour cream, onions, and liquid hot pepper seasoning. Pour into a large, shallow buttered casserole (about 3 qt. size); sprinkle cheese over the top. (At this point you can cover and chill casserole.) Bake in a 350° oven for 25 minutes. (If refrigerated, bake 15 minutes longer or until hot through.) Makes 18 servings.

Cherry Torte

    2   cups canned pitted sour cherries
    1/2 cup sugar
    2   tablespoons cornstarch
    1-1/4 cups regular all-purpose flour
    1/8 teaspoon salt
    1/2 teaspoon baking powder
    2   teaspoons sugar
    6   tablespoons each butter and shortening
    1   egg yolk
    2   tablespoons water
    2   egg whites
    1/8 teaspoon cream of tartar
    4   tablespoons sugar

Drain cherries and reserve 1/2 cup of the juice. Mix the 1/2 cup sugar and the cornstarch, add to cherries and reserved juice and cook, stirring, until thick; cool.

Sift flour with salt, baking powder, and the 2 teaspoons sugar into a bowl. Cut in butter and shortening with pastry blender or 2 knives until particles are of even size. Mix egg yolk with the 2 tablespoons water and stir into mixture to make a very stiff dough. Spread dough evenly in a 9-inch pie pan

Pour cold cherry sauce into torte shell. Bake in a 425° oven for 25 minutes. Meanwhile, beat egg whites with cream of tartar until foamy; gradually beat in the 4 tablespoons sugar; beat until stiff but not dry. Remove torte from oven after the 25 minutes and quickly spread with meringue, and return to oven. Turn heat down to 350° and bake 15 minutes longer, or until meringue is lightly browned. Serve warm or at room temperature. For 18 servings make 3 tortes.

Veal Birds for 10

SARDINE PÂTÉ WITH ITALIAN BREAD STICKS

ASPARAGUS SALAD

VEAL BIRDS WITH HERB SAUCE

CALABRIAN NOODLES

BABA AU RHUM WITH STRAWBERRIES

Veal birds in a full-flavored herb sauce make a very impressive entrée for a large gathering. Mild cheese-blended Calabrian noodles and fresh asparagus make delicious additions to the meal. (If fresh asparagus is not in season, substitute a green vegetable of your choice.) Every item on the menu except the noodles can be made ahead of time. The pâté can be made the day before the party and chilled. You can prepare the veal rolls up to the point of baking early in the day; cool and chill, then bake them just before serving. The Baba au Rhum can be made a day ahead.

Sardine Pâté

    2   large packages (8 oz. each) cream cheese
    3   tablespoons lemon juice
    2   tablespoons grated onion
    2   tablespoons minced parsley
    3   cans (4 oz. each) boneless sardines in oil
         Minced parsley for garnish
         Radishes

Mash cream cheese with lemon juice, onion, parsley, and sardines. When well blended, form into a mound and sprinkle with minced parsley. Surround with radishes. Cover and chill until time to serve. Makes 10 servings.

Asparagus Salad

4 pounds fresh asparagus, tough ends removed
  Boiling salted water
  Butter lettuce hearts
1/2 to 3/4 cup prepared oil and vinegar dressing

Cook the tender asparagus stems in a wide pan of boiling water to cover, uncovered, until easily pierced with a fork. Drain immediately and allow to cool to room temperature; do not chill if you want maximum asparagus flavor. At serving time, arrange on a platter, surround with tender hearts of butter lettuce, and pour over enough dressing to moisten. Makes 10 servings.

Veal Birds with Herb Sauce

4 pounds boneless veal cutlets, sliced thin
1 small onion
1/4 pound cooked ham
1-1/2 cups soft bread crumbs
2 tablespoons melted butter
1 teaspoon lemon juice
1 small clove garlic, minced
1/4 teaspoon thyme
2 tablespoons minced parsley
1 teaspoon salt
1/4 teaspoon pepper
  All-purpose flour
  Butter, margarine, or shortening

Sauce:

2 tablespoons each butter and all-purpose flour
1 cup each dry white wine and condensed consommé
  or chicken broth
1 tablespoon each minced parsley and chives
1/2 teaspoon each tarragon and thyme

Trim away tough membrane of veal. Then place veal pieces between sheets of waxed paper and flatten to about 1/4 inch thickness with a flat surfaced mallet. Cut in pieces about 2 by 3 inches and save the trimmings. Force trimmings, onion and ham through medium blade of a food chopper. Mix with bread crumbs, melted butter, lemon juice, garlic, thyme, parsley, salt, and pepper. Spread this mixture on the pieces of veal; roll and tie. Dust with flour and brown on all sides in shortening over medium-high heat in a frying pan. Place side by side in a close-fitting shallow baking dish. To make sauce melt butter in the pan used to brown veal, add flour and gradually blend in wine and consommé. Add parsley, chives, tarragon, and thyme. Bring to a boil, stirring; cook until thickened; pour over the veal rolls. (At this point you can cover and chill casserole.) Bake in a 350° oven until simmering, about 30 minutes (45 minutes, if refrigerated). Serve hot. Makes 10 servings.

Calabrian Noodles

1 pound ricotta cheese (or cottage cheese)
3/4 cup hot water
2 tablespoons olive oil
3 tablespoons melted butter
1 teaspoon salt
1/2 teaspoon freshly ground pepper
1 pound egg noodles

Combine cheese, water, oil, butter, salt and pepper; beat until smooth. Heat in top of double boiler over hot water. Cook noodles according to package directions; drain well, and mix with hot sauce. Serve at once. Makes 10 servings.

Baba Au Rhum

1/4 cup currants
1/2 cup scalded milk
1 package yeast, active dry or compressed
1/4 cup warm water (lukewarm for compressed yeast)
2 cups regular all-purpose flour, unsifted
4 eggs, well beaten
1/3 cup butter
2 tablespoons sugar
1/2 teaspoon salt
1 cup strained apricot preserves
1 cup water
1/2 cup rum or 1 teaspoon rum flavoring
  Sliced sugared strawberries
  Whipped cream (optional)

In a mixing bowl put currants in hot milk to plump and cool. Sprinkle or crumble in the yeast in the 1/4 cup water and let stand until softened. Add to cool milk along with the flour and eggs, and beat vigorously with a heavy spoon for 3 to 4 minutes. Allow to rise in a warm place until almost doubled in bulk. Cream butter, sugar, and salt together and beat into batter. Divide among 12 well-greased custard cups (about 8-oz. size). Allow to rise until doubled, then bake in a 400° oven for 15 minutes or until browned and a wooden skewer inserted in center comes out clean. Remove babas from cups and turn upside down onto a flat rimmed pan. Heat the strained apricot preserves with the 1 cup water; remove from heat; add rum. Pour sauce evenly over babas and let soak at room temperature for several hours, basting occasionally with sauce. Serve with sliced sugared strawberries and, if you wish, whipped cream. More rum may be poured over the babas before serving. Makes 12 servings.

Company Corned Beef Dinner for 18

FRUITED CORNED BEEF

HOT WHOLE APRICOTS

LIMA BEAN CASSEROLE

HOT POPPY SEED ROLLS

CHEESECAKE WITH SOUR CREAM TOPPING

The corned beef for this main dish may be cooked as much as two days in advance; let it cool and chill in its broth so it will retain its juiciness when oven browned to serve. A day ahead or the morning of the party, make the cheesecake; cool, and chill, but let it come to room temperature before serving. You can assemble the lima bean casserole in the morning and chill.

Fruited Corned Beef

9	pounds corned beef round (2 pieces, 4 to 5 pounds each)
	Water
	Whole cloves
1	cup firmly packed brown sugar
1/2	cup fine dry bread crumbs
1	teaspoon dry mustard
2	teaspoons grated orange peel
1	teaspoon grated lemon peel
1/2	cup orange juice
3	tablespoons lemon juice
2	cups apple cider

Cover meat with cold water, bring to a boil. If water tastes at all salty, pour off water and cover meat with fresh water; return to boil, covered. Simmer slowly for 4 hours, or until meat is tender to pierce; cool and chill in broth (as long as overnight). Transfer corned beef to close fitting pan and place fat side up. Score fat and stud with cloves. Combine brown sugar, crumbs, mustard, orange peel, and lemon peel. Pat meat with crumb mixture. Place in a 350° oven and bake until slightly browned, basting frequently with a mixture of the orange and lemon juices and cider. After browning, continue baking for 30 minutes or until heated through. Slice. Makes 18 servings.

Lima Bean Casserole

8	medium-sized onions, sliced
4	tablespoons (1/4 cup) butter or margarine
3	cans (4 oz. each) sliced mushrooms, drained
2	cans (10-1/2 oz. each) condensed cream of mushroom soup
6	packages (10 oz. each) frozen baby lima beans
	Boiling water
1	teaspoon salt
1/4	teaspoon pepper
2	teaspoons dill seed
1	pint (2 cups) whipping cream
2	cups grated or shredded Parmesan cheese

Sauté sliced onions in butter until limp. Stir in drained mushrooms and soup. Cook limas, uncovered, in boiling water (about 1/2 the depth of the beans), with salt, pepper, and dill seed for 5 minutes; drain. Combine limas and mushrooms with onion mixture in a greased large, shallow baking pan (about 4-qt. size); mix lightly. Pour over the cream and sprinkle the top with cheese. Bake in 350° oven for 45 minutes. Makes 18 servings.

Cheese Cake with Sour Cream Topping

6	large packages (8 oz. each) cream cheese
8	egg whites
2	cups sugar
2	teaspoons vanilla
1-1/3	cups finely crushed zwieback crumbs
2	pints (4 cups) sour cream
1/4	cup sugar
1	teaspoon vanilla
2/3	cup toasted, slivered blanched almonds

Cream cheese until soft. Beat egg whites until foamy and gradually add the 2 cups sugar, beating until stiff but not dry; mix part of the whites with the creamed cheese and the 2 teaspoons vanilla, stirring until blended; fold in the balance of the whites. Generously butter 2 cheesecake pans (8-inch diameter with removable bottom or spring released sides) and dust with the crumbs. Pour half the cheese mixture into each pan. Bake in a 350° oven for 25 minutes. Mix together the sour cream, the 1/4 cup sugar, and the 1 teaspoon vanilla, and spread equally over cheese filling. Sprinkle with almonds and return to a 475° oven for 5 minutes. Cool and chill thoroughly. Serve at room temperature. Makes 18 servings.

Roast Cornish Game Hen Dinner

ASSORTED RAW VEGETABLES

HERB DIP

CONSOMME WITH AVOCADO

ROAST CORNISH GAME HENS   FRIED RICE

PEAS WITH WATER CHESTNUTS

COFFEE ICE CREAM WITH
GRATED CHOCOLATE

This menu has so much flexibility that it can easily be adapted to accommodate any number of guests. It is simple to figure portions: For each person, plan on 3/4 cup consommé, 1 Rock Cornish game hen, and 1/2 cup of peas. One pint of ice cream serves 4 persons. You can prepare the relishes early in the day (keep crisp in ice water) and also make the herb dip and the fried rice stuffing, if you wish. Stuff the hens just before you roast them.

Assorted Raw Vegetables

Prepare an assortment of any or all of these allowing about 3/4 cup for each serving: carrot sticks, celery hearts, finocchio (fennel), raw asparagus, turnip sticks, green onions, radishes, green pepper strips, sliced cauliflower buds, raw mushrooms, sliced zucchini or cherry tomatoes. Serve with Herb Dip (recipe follows).

Herb Dip

1   large package (8 oz.) cream cheese at room temperature
1   cup (1/2 pint) sour cream
1   tablespoon each minced chives and parsley
1   teaspoon each minced fresh or crumbled dry tarragon, dill weed, soy sauce, and curry powder
     Milk

Mash the cream cheese with a fork and gradually, smoothly add sour cream. Blend in chives, parsley, tarragon, dill, soy sauce, and curry powder, and enough milk to make the dip soft enough to cling to vegetables but not runny. Cover and chill. Makes about 1-1/2 cups or enough for 8 servings.

Consommé with Avocado

Dilute (if desired) canned consommé according to label directions and heat to simmering. Ladle into bowls and add diced avocado (moisten lightly with lemon juice to preserve color if allowed to stand). Allow 3/4 cup consommé and 1/6 of an avocado for each serving.

Fried Rice

This may be used as a stuffing for the Rock Cornish hens or served as a separate vegetable.

1/2   pound thinly sliced mushrooms
3   tablespoons butter
4   cups hot or cold cooked rice
3   tablespoons salad oil
2   tablespoons minced green onions
1   teaspoon chopped fresh ginger
2   eggs
2   tablespoons soy sauce
      Salt
1/4   cup slivered almonds (optional)

In a wide frying pan, sauté mushrooms in butter until limp; set aside. In the frying pan cook rice in the oil for about 5 minutes over medium heat; stir while cooking. Add the mushrooms, green onions, and ginger, and cook for 3 minutes more; then break in the eggs and continue to cook and stir until the egg is set. Season

with the soy sauce and salt to taste. Add slivered almonds, if you wish. Serve at once or use to stuff 8 to 10 Cornish hens.

Roast Rock Cornish Game Hens

Thaw 1 Rock Cornish game hen (about 20 oz. size) for each serving. Remove giblets and reserve for other purposes. Rinse birds inside and out and pat dry. Fill cavities, if desired, with Fried Rice (recipe is above); you will need about 1/3 to 1/2 cup for each bird. Skewer cavities shut. Place breast up on a rimmed baking sheet. Bake in a 350° oven for 60 to 70 minutes or until leg joint moves easily.

Baste frequently with a blend of equal parts of soy sauce, Sherry, and salad oil (allow about 1 tablespoon for each bird).

Peas with Water Chestnuts

Cook frozen peas in boiling salted water until tender according to package directions; drain. Combine with sliced water chestnuts and butter. For each 2 cups of hot cooked peas add 4 tablespoons sliced water chestnuts and about 1 tablespoon butter; allow about 1/2 cup of peas for each serving.

Coffee Ice Cream with Grated Chocolate

Put scoops of coffee ice cream in chilled sherbet glasses. Sprinkle each serving with about 1 tablespoon of shaved semisweet or milk chocolate.

A Large Dinner

CREAM CONSOMMÉ

STRAWBERRY-BLUEBERRY MOLD

BAKED KOTLETI

CARROTS VICHY

BROWNED NEW POTATOES

BUTTERED BROCCOLI

SALZTANGERL

HIMMEL TORTE

Practically all of these dishes lend themselves to advance preparation, so you can be quite unhurried as you serve your guests. Each recipe is geared for 10. You can cook the soup, meatballs and mold the salad a day ahead. If you can find them, buy the *Salztangerl* (long slender rolls sprinkled with coarse salt and caraway seeds); or you can simply serve hot yeast rolls. Assemble the torte a few hours before serving; but you can bake the cake layers a day in advance.

Cream Consommé

    1   large onion
    1   tart apple, unpeeled
    3   cans (10-1/2 oz. each) condensed consommé
1-1/2   cups whipping cream
         Salt to taste
         Dash each paprika and curry powder
    1   red-skinned apple
         Juice of 1/2 lemon

Cook the onion in boiling water to cover for 10 minutes; drain. Grate the parboiled onion and the unpeeled apple; add to the consommé and cook until tender, about 10 minutes. Purée in a blender or force through a wire strainer. Stir in cream and season with salt, paprika, and curry powder. Reheat slowly, just until hot throughout. Serve in small cups, garnished with chopped red apple that you have sprinkled with lemon juice. Makes 10 servings.

Strawberry-Blueberry Mold

3-3/4 cups water
2 packages (3 oz. each) *wild cherry-flavored gelatin*
1/4 cup *dry Sherry*
  About 2 cups strawberries (1 basket)
1-1/2 cups fresh blueberries or 1 package (10 oz.) *frozen unsugared blueberries, practically thawed*
2 cans (1 lb. each) *seedless grapes, drained*
  Salad greens
  About 1/4 cup prepared oil and vinegar style *French dressing*

Heat 2 cups of the water, add flavored gelatin, and stir until dissolved. Stir in the remaining 1-3/4 cups water and the wine; chill until syrupy. Wash and halve strawberries, and arrange in the bottom of a 3-quart ring mold, or use individual molds. Pour in enough of the chilled gelatin to cover berries; set in ice water to mold quickly. Mix the remaining gelatin with blueberries and grapes, and pour into mold. Chill, covered, until firm. When ready to serve, immerse pan to rim in hot tap water to loosen salad. At once invert onto a platter lined with salad greens that have been moistened with French dressing. Makes 10 to 12 servings.

Baked Kotleti

3 pounds very lean ground beef
6 tablespoons butter or margarine
2 teaspoons salt
1/2 teaspoon freshly ground pepper
2 tablespoons minced parsley
6 slices stale bread
  Water
4 eggs, separated
4 tablespoons all-purpose flour
2 cups canned undiluted consommé
6 tablespoons sour cream
  Additional sour cream

Add to the ground meat 2 tablespoons softened butter, salt, pepper, and parsley. Soak bread in water, squeeze nearly dry, and tear up finely; add to the meat mixture, along with egg yolks; mix thoroughly. Whip egg whites until stiff, but not dry, and fold in, stirring with a fork. Form meat mixture into 2 dozen equal sized oval-shaped patties. Sauté in the remaining butter until browned on each side. Transfer to a casserole.

Stir flour into the drippings and brown slightly, then stir in consommé; bring to a boil. Stir in the 6 tablespoons sour cream, blending until smooth, and pour over the meatballs. Bake in a 350° oven for 25 minutes. Makes 10 servings. Accompany with additional sour cream to spoon onto individual servings.

Carrots Vichy

  About 12 (2 bunches) carrots
1/4 cup butter
2 tablespoons sugar
  Salt and pepper to taste
  Finely chopped parsley

Peel and thinly slice carrots. Melt butter in a wide frying pan, add carrots, sugar, salt, and pepper; cook, uncovered, over medium-high heat, stirring frequently until tender, about 10 to 12 minutes. Just before serving, sprinkle with finely chopped parsley. Makes 10 servings.

Himmel Torte

Himmel Torte is German for Heavenly Tart, and this dessert deserves the name. It is six layers of crisp butter cooky, spread with a tart jelly and whipped cream.

1-1/2 cups (3/4 lb.) butter or margarine
3/4 cup granulated sugar
3 egg yolks
1 whole egg
2-1/4 cups all-purpose flour
3/4 cup currant jelly
1 cup (1/2 pt.) whipping cream
  Powdered sugar

Cream butter and gradually add the granulated sugar, creaming until light and fluffy. Beat in egg yolks, one at a time; add whole egg and beat until smooth. Sift flour, measure, and gradually mix into the creamed mixture. Using a spatula, spread dough equally in a thin even layer over the bottom of six 8-inch, round layer pans (or use 3 pans and bake cake in 2 batches). Bake in a 375° oven for 12 to 15 minutes, or until the cakes are golden brown on the edges. Turn out of pans and let cool. Spread 5 of the cake layers with currant jelly. Whip cream until stiff, sweeten to taste with powdered sugar. Spread the currant coated cake layers equally with cream; stack layers and top with the remaining plain cake layer. Sift powdered sugar over it. Chill until ready to serve. Makes 12 servings.

Chafing Dish Party

A few large chafing dishes simplify elegant service. If possible have the beef stroganoff in one chafing dish, the rice in another, and the carrots in still another.

Melon and Ginger Cocktail

Use 3 or 4 varieties of melons. Cut the melons in balls or in cylinders. (Use an apple corer and cut the resulting pieces in uniform lengths.)

1-1/2	cups sugar
1/4	cup white corn syrup
1/2	cup water
2	tablespoons grated ginger
2	tablespoons lime or lemon juice
2	quarts melon balls or cylinders
	Mint sprigs
6	small cantaloupes, cut in halves and seeded (optional)

Blend sugar, syrup, water, and ginger; bring to a boil and simmer, uncovered for 6 minutes. Cool and add lime or lemon juice. Pour over melon balls and chill at least 1 hour. Serve in sherbet glasses or, if preferred, in halves of small cantaloupes, and garnish with a sprig of mint. Makes 12 servings.

Beef Stroganoff

4	pounds top round steak, sliced 1/2 inch thick
2	cups sliced onions
1/2	cup (1/4 lb.) butter
1	pound mushrooms, sliced
1	cup condensed canned bouillon (may be half dry white wine)
3	cups (1-1/2 pts.) sour cream
	Salt, pepper, and prepared mustard to taste
	Hot cooked rice

Pound the steak until very thin with a flat surfaced mallet between sheets of waxed paper, then cut in pieces about 3 inches long and 1/2 inch wide. Cook the onion in the butter in a large frying pan until wilted. Then add the mushrooms and the beef, and cook for 5 minutes over high heat, stirring. Pour in the bouillon and cover. Simmer about 45 minutes or until the meat is tender and the liquid almost evaporated. Stir in the sour cream, season to taste with salt, pepper, and mustard, and heat gently but do not boil. Spoon over hot cooked rice. Makes 12 servings.

Carrots in Wine Sauce

16	medium-sized carrots, scraped and sliced
	Water
1	teaspoon salt
1/2	cup minced onion
1	clove garlic
2	tablespoons butter
2	tablespoons all-purpose flour
1	cup undiluted canned consommé
1/2	cup dry white wine
	Salt and pepper

Cover and simmer carrots until tender in a small amount of water with the 1 teaspoon salt; drain. Sauté onion and garlic in melted butter until golden brown; then discard garlic. Stir flour into sautéed onions, then gradually stir in consommé and wine; cook, stirring constantly, until thickened. Add cooked carrots to the sauce; cover and reheat until bubbly. Season to taste with salt and pepper. Makes 12 servings.

Hot Herb Bread

1	cup (1/2 lb.) butter
3/4	cup each minced chives and parsley
1/4	cup minced fresh basil or 2 tablespoons dry basil, crumbled
2	large loaves French bread, split lengthwise

Cream together butter, chives, parsley, and sweet basil. Place loaves, cut side up, 6 inches below broiler; heat and toast lightly. Spread hot bread evenly with butter. Cut in 2-inch pieces. Makes 12 servings.

Baked Strawberry Alaska

    2-quart brick vanilla ice cream
1   layer (8-inch) sponge or pound cake
2   cups sliced sugared strawberries
6   egg whites
1/4 teaspoon cream of tartar
1   cup sugar

Put heavy foil on a board slightly larger than the cake; place cake on foil. Put the ice cream on the cake and hollow out the center of the ice cream enough to pour in the strawberries. Spread surplus ice cream over the opening and put in the freezer while you make the meringue. Beat the egg whites with the cream of tartar until stiff, then beat in sugar gradually and continue beating until very stiff. Spread the meringue over the ice cream and cake, covering it completely. Bake in a preheated oven (450°) until nicely browned, about 5 minutes. Serve at once, with more sliced strawberries, if desired. Makes 12 servings.

Brisket Dinner

RAW MUSHROOM SALAD WITH
CHEDDAR CHEESE

BUTTERED WHOLE WHEAT TOAST TRIANGLES

BAKED BRISKET WITH PAN SAUCE

BAKED POTATOES

ITALIAN GREEN BEANS

CHOCOLATE ECLAIRS   FROZEN RASPBERRIES

Start the brisket 8 hours before you plan to serve it. Bake 1 medium-sized potato (about 4 oz. each) for each guest with the brisket the last 2-1/2 hours it cooks. Plan on 3 to 4 packages frozen Italian green beans to serve 10 to 12 guests. For dessert top chocolate frosted eclairs (frozen, bakery made, or homemade) with thawed frozen raspberries and their syrup.

Raw Mushroom Salad with Cheddar Cheese

3/4 pound mushrooms
1   small mild onion (red, if available)
4   tablespoons each wine vinegar and olive oil or salad oil
1   tablespoon minced parsley
1/2 teaspoon each basil, dry mustard, and sugar
    About 1/4 pound sharp Cheddar cheese
6   to 8 medium-sized romaine lettuce leaves
    Buttered whole wheat toast triangles (optional)

Trim stem ends from mushrooms and slice thinly through caps. Also thinly slice onion and separate rings. Combine vinegar, oil, parsley, basil, mustard, and sugar and mix gently with mushrooms and onions. Cover and chill at least 30 minutes or as long as 4 to 5 hours before serving.

Slice cheese as thinly as possible. Group all on a flat serving dish laced in romaine leaves and mound the mushroom mixture on one end and the cheese slices on the other end. Serve accompanied by toast triangles. Makes 10-12 small servings.

Baked Brisket with Pan Sauce

6   to 7-pound piece well trimmed fresh beef brisket
1/3 cup each lemon juice (freshly squeezed) and firmly packed brown sugar
1/2 cup catsup
1   tablespoon Dijon-style or brown mustard
3   tablespoons Worcestershire
1   teaspoon salt
2   tablespoons each cornstarch and water

Lay meat flat in a baking pan; rim should be higher than meat surface. Blend lemon juice, sugar, catsup, mustard, Worcestershire, and salt. Pour over meat. Cover and bake in a 300° oven for 6 hours. If covered with foil, do not let meat touch foil during cooking.

After 6 hours, remove cover and bake another 1 to 1-1/2 hours, basting frequently with juices, until meat pierces readily. Keep warm on carving board. Skim off as much fat as possible from pan juices. Bring juices to boiling; blend cornstarch with water to a smooth paste; gradually stir into boiling sauce until thick. Amount used depends on quantity of pan juices. Slice brisket thinly; spoon sauce over portions. Makes 10 to 12 servings.

Easy Entertaining

...Buffets

*T*o serve a meal buffet style doesn't necessarily mean that the foods are lined up in an orderly fashion on a buffet, nor do the foods to be offered necessarily have to include a first course through dessert.

The menus in this chapter demonstrate just how adaptable buffet service can be. The dishes featured tend to be ones that serve attractively at room temperature or can be reheated and held hot on warming trays or in chafing dishes; the majority can be made well ahead of time.

These menus will serve a modest 6 to 8 or 50. In the housewarming party for 50, you group foods that go together in various locations, inviting guests to wander to and from each post, in any order that suits their fancy. The sandwich buffet for 12 to 16 is handled in a similar manner, yet is so simple you can have it ready to serve in less than 2 hours. Both parties keep the need for utensils at an absolute minimum.

The smörgåsbord follows a more traditional menu pattern, but is designed to be suitable for brunch, lunch or supper. The smaller buffets feature such varied entrées as meat and vegetable fritters, barbecued chicken with fruit curry, and a lamb and beef loaf with interesting vegetable accompaniments.

This candlelit smörgåsbord buffet table offers a bounteous selection of cheese, fish, breads, meats, and salads. Decorative serving containers add a festive touch. Menu and recipes can be found on pages 32 - 34.

Western Smörgåsbord

FISH: HERRING IN SPICES, HERRING IN SOUR
CREAM, ANCHOVY SPRATS, SMOKED
SALMON WITH EGG AND ONION,
SHRIMP PYRAMID

MEATS: MEATBALLS, BAKED HAM WITH CRAB
APPLES, ASSORTED COLD CUTS

SALADS: PICKLED FRESH CUCUMBERS,
COLESLAW WITH APPLE

CHEESES: SWEDISH SVEA-OST, NORWEGIAN
JARLSBERG, DANISH BLUE

BREADS: KNACKE BREAD (KNÄCKEBRÖD)
AND LEFSE

CONDIMENTS: PRESERVED LINGONBERRIES,
MUSTARDS

DESSERT: COFFEE, NORWEGIAN LACE
COOKIES, SWEDISH SPRITZ, APPLES

A party buffet like this is flexible enough for many occasions—from brunch through dinner or late supper—for a varied number of guests. Your smörgåsbord will be an effortless undertaking if you take advantage of the large selection of ready-to-eat Scandinavian delicacies in supermarkets, delicatessens, and specialty food shops. Or if you prefer, make some of the dishes yourself. This menu is a guide to serving 24 guests.

For the Fish:

Buy 1 jar (about 12 oz. *each*) herring in spices and herring in sour cream, and 1 can (8 oz.) anchovy sprats, and 1 pound thinly sliced smoked salmon (lox). Next to the salmon arrange for serving, finely chopped onion and separate mounds sieved hard-cooked egg yolks and egg whites. These condiments are piled on a salmon slice and rolled up when eaten.

For the shrimp pyramid, buy 2 pounds large shrimp, cooked, shelled, and deveined. Mound shrimp in a bowl and nest in another bowl filled with crushed ice. Serve with skewers or toothpicks for eating.

For the Meats:

You can make the Scandinavian style meatballs or buy 6 cans (15 oz. *each*) meatballs and heat in their own gravy with 1 cup sour cream; serve from a chafing dish.

Scandinavian Meatballs

    Instant mashed potatoes
4   pounds lean ground beef
1   envelope (about 1-3/8 oz. or for 4 servings) dehydrated onion soup mix
4   eggs
1   cup milk
1/2 cup quick-cooking rolled oats
1/3 cup finely chopped parsley
3/4 teaspoon nutmeg
1/4 cup each *butter or margarine and all-purpose flour*
1   pint (2 cups) milk or half-and-half
1   teaspoon salt
1   cup sour cream

Prepare enough instant mashed potatoes to make 1 cup, adding water, milk, and seasoning as directed on the package. If you have a heavy-duty electric mixer, use it; otherwise use your hands for mixing the following in a large bowl; ground beef, soup mix, eggs, milk, potatoes, rolled oats, parsley, and 1/2 teaspoon of the nutmeg. Mix until smoothly blended. Shape into 1-1/4-inch balls and place 1 inch apart on shallow baking pans. Bake in a 450° oven for 10 minutes, or until well browned. Transfer to a shallow serving casserole, reserving the pan drippings.

For sour cream gravy, melt butter in a saucepan until bubbly and blend in flour; cook a few minutes until flour mixture turns golden brown. Stir in milk and, stirring constantly, cook until thickened. Add reserved drippings, salt, remaining 1/4 teaspoon nutmeg, and sour cream, stirring to blend.

Spoon sauce over meatballs. (At this point you may let cool to room temperature, cover, and refrigerate until serving time—as long as a day ahead.) Bake in a 350° oven, uncovered, for about 25 minutes (35 minutes if refrigerated), or until hot through. Makes about 12 to 16 servings.

Ham

Buy a 6-pound or larger canned ham or whole or half a butt or shank ham. Bake as the package directs, a day in advance if you wish. Serve warm or cold.

Assorted cold cuts can be used with or in place of the ham. Include about 24 slices Danish salami, 12 slices head cheese, and 24 slices smoked beef.

For Salads:

Buy 1 quart marinated fresh cucumbers and 2 quarts coleslaw or make the following.

Pickled Fresh Cucumbers

> About 4 medium-sized cucumbers
> 1 tablespoon salt
> 1/2 cup tarragon-flavored wine vinegar
> 1/4 cup water
> 1-1/2 tablespoons sugar
> 1/8 teaspoon freshly ground pepper
> 1/2 teaspoon dill weed
> 3 tablespoons finely chopped parsley

Score unpeeled cucumbers with a fork, or peel them. Slice very thin to make 8 cups and layer into a bowl, sprinkling each layer with part of the salt. Cover and chill 2 to 3 hours; then drain and rinse thoroughly with cold water and drain again. Mix together the vinegar, water, sugar, pepper, dill, and parsley. Pour over the sliced cucumbers and mix well. Chill until serving time (you can make it a day in advance). Makes 12 servings.

Coleslaw with Apple

> 1 large head cabbage
> 3 red-skinned apples (Winesap or Delicious)
> 1 cup whipping cream
> 1 cup sour cream
> 1/3 cup white wine vinegar
> 1-1/2 tablespoons sugar
> 1/2 teaspoon salt
> Freshly ground pepper
> 1 can (13-1/2 oz.) pineapple tidbits, drained (optional)
> Juice of 1/2 lemon

Finely shred enough cabbage to make 2 quarts. Coarsely shred 2 of the unpeeled apples and add to the cabbage.

For the dressing, mix together the whipping cream, sour cream, vinegar, sugar, salt, and pepper to taste, and pour over the cabbage mixture. If a sweet coleslaw is desired, add the pineapple tidbits.

Place in a serving bowl, cover, and chill until serving time (up to 12 hours). Just before serving, slice remaining unpeeled apple; brush the cut surfaces with lemon juice. Arrange apple slices in a pinwheel in the center of the salad. Makes 12 servings.

For the Cheeses:

Purchase 2 pounds each of Swedish svea-ost and Norwegian Jarlsberg and 1 pound of Danish Blue.

For the Breads:

Buy 2 packages (about 1 lb.) of the large round crisp knäckebröd and 2 packages (13 oz. each) lefse, or make your own lefse.

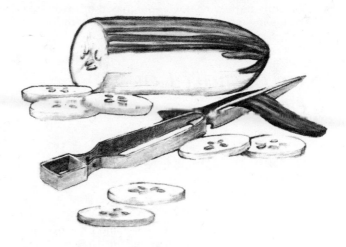

Lefse

> 3-1/2 cups regular all-purpose flour
> 3 teaspoons baking powder
> 1/2 teaspoon salt
> 1/4 cup sugar
> 1-1/2 teaspoons soda
> 1-1/2 cups buttermilk
> Salad oil

Sift the flour, measure 2-1/2 cups, and sift it with the baking powder, salt, and sugar into a large bowl. Mix soda and buttermilk until foamy and add to flour mixture. With an electric mixer beat at medium speed for 5 minutes until batter is satiny and smooth. Measure remaining 1 cup sifted flour and mix into batter, using a dough hook or a wooden spoon, until it becomes smoothly mixed.

Cover bowl tightly and refrigerate for at least 1 hour.

To cook lefse, preheat an electric griddle or electric frying pan to 375°, or use a large frying pan over medium heat. Spread a pastry cloth or a dish towel on a board and flour it; also cover your rolling pin with stockinet and flour it well. Remove half the dough at a time from the refrigerator, form it into a cylinder, then divide into 16 pieces of equal size.

With floured hands, shape each piece of dough into a ball, flatten it to an even circle on the cloth, flour dough well on both sides, then roll out to about 6 inches in diameter, keeping cloth well floured. Lightly grease the griddle, using a crumpled paper towel dipped in salad oil. Shake excess flour off each cake and put onto griddle. It should start to bubble immediately. Cook until bubbles are lightly browned, about 1-1/2 minutes; turn and brown other side. Repeat rolling and baking until all are done.

Cool and stack cakes, wrap well and store at room temperature up to 1 week or freeze.

If you want to serve lefse warm sprinkle each one lightly with water then stack 16 together at a time, seal in foil and warm in a 300° oven for 10 to 15 minutes. Makes 32 lefse.

For Dessert:

Accompany buttery cookies—purchased or made from the following recipes—with a basket filled with 2 dozen shiny red apples.

Norwegian Lace Cookies

1/2	cup (1/4 lb.) butter or margarine
1-1/2	cups regular rolled oats
1	egg
2/3	cup sugar
1	teaspoon baking powder
1	tablespoon all-purpose flour

Melt the butter in a small saucepan and pour over the oatmeal, placed in a bowl. Beat egg until light and beat in the sugar. Mix together the baking powder and flour and stir into the egg mixture along with the oatmeal mixture. Drop level tablespoonsful of batter onto a greased and floured baking sheet, 2 or 3 inches apart.

Bake in a 375° oven for 10 minutes or until golden brown. Remove from the oven and let stand on baking sheets about 1 minute. Then quickly lift cookies (they should still be hot and flexible) with a spatula. Drape over foil-covered broom handle; press gently into saddle shape. When cool, lift off. Makes about 2 dozen.

Swedish Spritz

1	cup (1/2 lb.) butter or margarine
3/4	cup sugar
3	egg yolks
2-1/2	cups all-purpose flour, unsifted
1/2	teaspoon baking powder
1/4	teaspoon almond extract
1	teaspoon vanilla

Beat the butter until creamy. Gradually add sugar, beating until fluffy. Add egg yolks, one at a time, and beat until smooth. Sift flour with baking powder and gradually add to the creamed mixture, mixing until well blended. Add almond extract and vanilla; mix well.

Place in a cooky press and push out dough on greased baking sheets, making small rings. Bake in a 350° oven 12 minutes or until light brown. Transfer hot cookies to cool on wire rack. Makes 5 dozen.

(If you don't have a cooky press follow recipe above but reduce flour to 2 cups. Pulverize 3 ounces blanched almonds in a blender to make 1/2 cup ground nuts and add to dough with flour. Shape into 3/4-inch balls. Press down on a greased baking sheet with bottom of juice glass dipped in sugar. Bake as directed above.)

Brazilian Feijoada Buffet

BRAZILIAN RICE   SAUTÉED GREENS

FEIJOADA (BEANS WITH ASSORTED MEATS)

SLICED ORANGES

TOASTED WHEAT TOPPING

LEMON CHILE SAUCE

FRESH PEARS AND GRAPES

In the traditional Brazilian menu, called *feijoada* (fay-zhwa-da) *completa*, each side dish plays a special role. In this feast of pungent meats and beans stew it is the rice that mellows the flavors. Fresh orange slices and briefly cooked greens provide refreshing accents. You spoon a tangy fresh lemon chile sauce liberally over the whole dish and then sprinkle on a toasted wheat topping. Consider serving jugs of California Barbera or Zinfandel to match the emphatic flavors of feijoada.

It's easier than you might expect to stage this kind of party. No special utensils are required except a pot that can hold at least 10 quarts. You can serve 12 people very well with this make-ahead dinner.

Get a head start on cooking the feijoada by pre-cooking the tongue, browning the sausages and spareribs, and soaking the beans a day ahead. You may have to order pigs' feet ahead, too. Toast the wheat topping a day or more ahead; Brazilians toast manioc flour for this, and you might possibly find it in a Mexican market. If not, use farina. Early on the day of the party, prepare the chile sauce and slice the oranges; keep both covered in the refrigerator. Precook the rice and prepare the greens for cooking.

Brazilian Rice

3	cups long grain rice, cooked according to package directions
1/4	cup each salad oil and butter
1	large onion, finely chopped
3	cloves garlic, minced or mashed
2	tomatoes, peeled, seeded, and chopped

Cook rice ahead, if convenient, and set aside until time to complete this dish. Heat oil and butter in a wide frying pan over medium heat. Sauté onion until golden. Add garlic and rice; cook, stirring, for 5 minutes. Stir in tomatoes. Reduce heat to warm and cover until serving time; it can be held at a warm temperature up to 1 hour. Makes 12 servings.

Sautéed Greens

2-1/2 pounds spinach or kale, thoroughly washed and drained
1/4 cup reserved drippings from cooking spareribs (see Feijoada recipe or use salad oil)
2 cloves garlic, minced or mashed
1/2 teaspoon salt
1 cup regular strength chicken broth

Trim off stems of greens and discard. Stack 10 to 15 spinach leaves or 5 to 10 kale leaves at a time and roll lengthwise into a tight bundle. Cut across the roll to make 1/4-inch-wide strips. Refrigerate well covered.

In a large frying pan, heat drippings over medium heat. Add garlic, salt, chicken broth, and as many greens as the pan will hold. Cook and stir, adding remaining greens as they can be fitted into the pan until all are wilted, about 5 minutes. Serve immediately if using spinach. For kale, cover, reduce heat to low, and simmer 15 minutes. Makes 12 servings.

Feijoada

1 small (about 3 lbs.) smoked beef tongue
4 pigs' feet cut in quarters (optional)
Water
1/2 teaspoon pepper
2 large onions, chopped
1 clove garlic, minced or mashed
2 whole bay leaves
2 pounds spareribs, cut into 12 pieces (if necessary, have longest ribs cut in halves)
1 pound pork link sausages
2 pounds (4-1/2 cups) regular kidney beans or 4 cups black beans (the kidney shaped ones, not the round Oriental black bean)
1 pound piece boneless lean beef chuck (the chuck fillet, also called Jewish fillet, is easiest to slice)
3 Portuguese or Polish sausages (about 3/4 lb.), cut in 1/2-inch slices
1 pound piece Canadian bacon or lean ham
1 whole orange, unpeeled
Salt to taste

Scrub the tongue under running water and rinse pigs' feet. In a 10-quart kettle, combine tongue, pigs' feet, 2-1/2 quarts water, pepper, onions, garlic, and bay leaves. Cover and bring to boiling; reduce heat and simmer 2 hours or until tongue is fork tender. Remove tongue, leaving pigs' feet in the pot. When tongue cools enough to handle, peel off skin and cut away fatty portions; set aside.

Arrange spareribs in a large shallow baking pan and bake in a 450° oven for 25 minutes. Distribute link sausages in the pan and continue baking 15 to 20 minutes, until well browned; remove, drain, and reserve drippings.

Pick out any foreign material from beans. Wash beans and add to the cooking pot with the pigs' feet, bring to a boil and boil for 2 minutes. Remove from heat, cover, and soak 1 hour. (Or you can omit the 2-minute boil and soak bean mixture overnight in refrigerator; also refrigerate all the meats.)

About 2 to 3 hours before dinner, heat bean mixture to boiling again. Add beef, Portuguese or Polish sausages, bacon, and whole orange. Cover and simmer 1 hour and 15 minutes or until beans and beef are almost tender. (If you use black beans, cook bean mixture 30 minutes before adding meats.) Every 15 or 20 minutes, stir gently and add boiling water to keep beans covered.

Remove orange and discard. Put into the kettle the cooked tongue, spareribs, and link sausages. Continue to simmer about 15 minutes or until heated through. Salt to taste.

To serve, remove link sausages and spareribs to a heated platter. Lift the tongue, beef, and bacon from the kettle; slice and arrange on the platter. Drizzle about 1/2 cup liquid from the beans over the meats. (You can hold the meats up to 1 hour on a covered platter in a 300° oven; keep the bean mixture warm, covered, on very low heat.) Serve bean mixture in a large bowl or soup tureen. Makes 12 servings.

Sliced Oranges

Cut and peel all white membrane from 6 large oranges. Slice oranges crosswise. If done ahead, cover and refrigerate.

Toasted Wheat Topping

Melt 1/2 cup (1/4 lb.) butter or margarine in a heavy frying pan over medium-high heat. Stir in 1 cup quick-cooking farina or manioc flour and 1/2 teaspoon salt. Cook and stir for 5 to 8 minutes or until cereal is light brown. Keep tightly covered until ready to use.

Lemon Chile Sauce

2 cups fresh lemon juice
2 small onions, finely chopped
4 cloves garlic, minced
2 medium-sized tomatoes, peeled, seeded, and chopped
2 teaspoons green salsa jalapeña or 1 can (4 oz.) California green chiles, seeded and finely chopped

Blend together the lemon juice, onions, garlic, tomatoes, and chiles. Cover and refrigerate up to 8 hours before serving. Makes 1 quart, enough for 12 servings.

Housewarming Party

COLD PLATTERS: CHOPPED CHICKEN LIVERS

BEEF TARTARE LOAF

SPREADS: MEAT TRAY

FISH TRAY

CHEESE TRAY

BREAD TRAY

HOT FOODS: GARLIC PORK NUGGETS

FONDUE BOURGUIGNONNE

CHINESE MEATBALLS

FONDUE NEUFCHATELOISE

Here's a party with lots of people, an abundance of good food—and almost no dishes to wash afterward. Finger food is the key to the flexibility and simplicity of the party. Whether 50 guests arrive for a cocktail party, for a buffet supper, or for the evening, they'll find refreshments to suit them. The buffet is planned for a minimum of preparation as well as for ease of service and clean-up. Included are some delicacies that can be prepared ahead and some "skewer" specialties that can be kept warmed or cooked in chafing dishes or electric frying pans. But the backbone of the menu

is an array of cold foods that you can purchase ready to serve; a meat tray, a cheese tray, and fish tray. Before guests arrive, arrange platters of the cold food on a buffet table, and place the hot foods at strategic spots throughout the party area.

Chopped Chicken Livers

This creamy pâté is especially delicious on rye bread. Many meat markets sell chicken fat; use it if possible, since it adds to the flavor; however, if you can't obtain it, substitute butter.

8   large onions, minced
1   cup chicken fat
3   pounds chicken livers
8   hard-cooked eggs, chopped
     Salt and pepper

In a wide frying pan cook onions until lightly browned in the chicken fat. Add chicken livers; cook until they have lost most of their pinkness. Cool slightly and chop rather fine. Add chopped hard-cooked eggs and salt and pepper to taste. If the mixture is not moist enough, add more chicken fat or butter to make a good spreading consistency. Makes 50 servings.

Beef Tartare Loaf

To be authentic, the raw beef should be scraped for this spread; if you don't have that kind of patience, trim off fat and grind the beef, using a fine blade of your food chopper. Spread on crackers, buttered French bread or dark pumpernickel.

5   pounds sirloin or other tender beef, trimmed of all fat and connective tissue, ground
4 or 5 egg yolks, slightly beaten
3   medium-sized onions, finely minced
5   teaspoons salt
1   teaspoon freshly ground pepper
1/2   cup minced parsley
       Chives
       Capers

Mix beef with egg yolks, onions, salt, pepper, and parsley. When thoroughly blended, form in a loaf or long roll and sprinkle with minced chives. Stud with whole capers. Keep cool to serve. (Nest tray in ice or serve a portion at a time, keeping the balance refrigerated.) Makes about 50 servings.

Meat Tray

You can prepare some of the meats at home, or buy them all, sliced, from a delicatessen; turkey, roast beef, ham, smoked tongue, and corned beef. Choose popular sausages such as salami, cervelat, and Braunschweiger.

For 50 people, count on a total of 5 pounds of meat. Serve with a bowl of mustard and a bowl of horseradish sauce (1 part prepared horseradish to 3 or 4 parts sour cream).

Fish Tray

A good selection is smoked salmon, kippered sturgeon, smoked Alaska cod (sablefish), smoked whitefish, sardines. If you prefer, serve a whole half smoked salmon with a very sharp slicing knife. Decorate the fish tray with lemon wedges, or place a bowl nearby. About 5 pounds of smoked fish will serve 50 guests.

Cheese Tray

Include mild cheese such as jack, Teleme, Swiss, or mild Cheddar, and sharp ones such as aged Cheddar and Port Salut. Serve at least one veined cheese, such as Roquefort, or blue cheese. An Edam or Gouda makes an attractive centerpiece for a cheese tray. Scoop out the insides to eat. Arrange other cheese on large leaves around the Edam or Gouda. You will need about 3 pounds of cheese for 50 servings.

Bread Tray

Provide one loaf each of three or four kinds of bread; rye, pumpernickel, a crusty French bread, and a whole wheat are good choices. Arrange bread, sliced and buttered, in overlapping layers on a large tray. Leave a few slices unbuttered for those who might prefer them that way.

Garlic Pork Nuggets

Eat these rich, crispy chunks of pork as they are, or dip them in a bowl of prepared taco sauce. Pork shoulder is an especially good cut to use for this dish.

5   pounds lean boneless pork
1   tablespoon salt
3   cloves garlic, puréed
     Freshly ground pepper

Cut pork into 1-inch cubes; mix thoroughly with salt and garlic and sprinkle with pepper. Spread in single layers in shallow baking pans, and bake in a 350° oven for 1 hour. Stir occasionally and drain off fat as it accumulates. When serving, reheat about a pound at a time in the 350° oven. Serve from a chafing dish. Makes enough for 50 servings.

Fondue Bourguignonne

Guests can choose from several sauces into which they can dip the skewered meat. Beef tenderloin is a good meat for this dish. Liver, kidney, sweetbreads, chicken breast, lamb, large peeled shrimp, and fish cubes are other alternatives. Do not cook meat and fish in the same fat.

      About 5 pounds meat or fish
      Butter
      Salad oil
2   dozen French rolls, sliced like bread

Cut meat into bite-sized chunks and heap, uncooked, into serving bowls. Put 1-1/2 inches of melted butter and salad oil in equal parts into electric saucepan, fondue pot, or chafing dish with a good heating element. Arrange around the container of meat, skewers or fondue forks, a selection of sauces (recipes follow), and a platter of French roll slices. Keep oil hot (375°) so meat will take only a couple of minutes to cook. Makes 50 servings.

Anchovy Sauce:

Add 2 tablespoons anchovy paste to 2 cups mayonnaise; mix well.

Bearnaise Sauce:

    6   green onions or shallots, minced
    1/4 cup wine vinegar
    4   egg yolks
    2   teaspoons dried tarragon
    1/4 teaspoon each salt and dry mustard
         Dash liquid hot pepper seasoning
    1   cup (1/2 lb.) melted butter

Cook green onions in wine vinegar until liquid is evaporated. Put in electric blender with egg yolks, tarragon, salt, mustard, and liquid hot pepper seasoning. Turn on blender for 5 seconds; gradually add melted butter. The sauce will thicken at once. If too thick, add a small amount of hot water.

Garlic Sauce:

Cream 1 pound soft butter with 2 minced or mashed cloves of garlic; add cayenne or Worcestershire to taste.

Sour Cream Sauce:

Add 2 tablespoons paprika and 1/4 cup very finely minced onion to 2 cups sour cream. Add salt to taste. Dill weed may be used instead of paprika.

Mustard Sauce:

Combine 2 cups mayonnaise, 2 tablespoons tarragon vinegar, and 3 tablespoons dry mustard. Mix well and add salt to taste.

Curry Sauce:

    2   tablespoons curry powder
    1   clove garlic, minced or mashed
    1   tablespoon lemon juice
    2   cans (10-1/2 oz. each) beef gravy

Combine curry powder, garlic, lemon juice, and gravy. Serve hot and keep warm.

Chinese Meatballs

These tiny meatballs, fried in deep fat before the party, simmer in a flavorful glaze in a chafing dish.

    2   cans (20 oz. each) water chestnuts
    3   bunches green onions (about 24) including most of
         the tops
    5   pounds lean pork, ground
    1/4 cup soy sauce
    6   eggs, slightly beaten
    1   tablespoon salt
    2-1/2 cups fine dry bread crumbs
         Cornstarch
         Salad oil for frying

Sauce:

    1   cup vinegar
    2   cups pineapple juice
    3/4 cup sugar
    2   cups canned undiluted consommé
    2   tablespoons soy sauce
    3   tablespoons grated fresh ginger (or 5 tablespoons
         chopped crystallized ginger)
    1/2 cup cornstarch
    1   cup cold water

Drain and chop water chestnuts; chop green onions, tops and all; mix both with meat. Add soy sauce, eggs, salt, and bread crumbs; mix thoroughly with your hands. Chill. Form into balls, using a rounded teaspoon for each; roll lightly in cornstarch. Fry in 2 inches salad oil heated to 370° until well browned.

To make sauce, heat together vinegar, pineapple juice, sugar, consommé, soy sauce, and ginger. Gradually blend cornstarch smoothly with cold water then add to sauce. Cook, stirring, until clear and thickened. Keep meatballs hot in chafing dish. Moisten with just enough sauce to form a slight glaze. Makes about 50 servings when served with other food.

Fondue Neufchateloise

Since this classic dish is best if made in fairly small batches, this recipe serves about 20 people when accompanied by the other foods. If you wish, have on hand additional shredded cheese and extra ingredients in proportional amounts to make batches of fondue in sequence.

    1   clove garlic, peeled
    5   cups dry white wine (such as Sylvaner or Grey
         Riesling)
    2-1/2 pounds Switzerland Swiss cheese, shredded
    1/2 tablespoon all-purpose flour
    1   teaspoon salt
         About 1/4 teaspoon ground nutmeg
    1/2 cup kirsch, cognac, or light rum
         Fresh ground pepper
    2   large loaves French bread, cut in bite-size cubes

Rub a 2-quart (or larger) earthenware fondue dish with garlic; add wine and heat over direct flame of chafing dish burner. Lightly mix the cheese with the flour; when the bubbles in the wine begin to rise to the surface, add the cheese mixture a handful at a time, stirring until each handful melts. Continue until all cheese is melted. Add salt, nutmeg, and kirsch, and stir well. Turn heat low but keep fondue slowly bubbling. Season with pepper to taste. Provide long-handled fondue forks or sturdy bamboo skewers. Each guest impales a bread cube and dunks it into the fondue. If the fondue becomes too thick, add a little heated wine. Makes 20 servings.

Assemble-Your-Own Sandwich Buffet

RYE AND BLUE CHEESE BOARD

BACON AND CHEESE PLATTER

ROAST BEEF BOARD

ARTICHOKE AND SALMON TRAY

You can shop and have this buffet for 12 to 16 guests ready to serve in an hour and a half or less. Once each of the four sandwich groupings is arranged—perhaps on trays, such as in several inviting locations in one or two rooms—it is a delight for the hostess because the guests assemble their own sandwiches at their own pace.

Rye and Blue Cheese Board

Present in separate containers slices of petite rye bread, blue cheese spread (recipe follows), and 1 to 2 bunches radishes, thinly sliced. Spread cheese on rounds of bread and top with radish slices.

Blue Cheese Spread:

1/2   cup (1/4 lb.) butter or margarine
1/2   pound (8 oz.) blue cheese
1/4   cup sour cream

Cream smoothly the butter with blue cheese in a bowl. Then blend in the sour cream. Chill, covered, as long as a week, until ready to serve. Makes about 1-2/3 cups.

Bacon and Cheese Platter

Set out on a large tray or board about 1 pound cooked Canadian bacon (sliced or a piece), about 1 pound jack cheese (unsliced), 1 or 2 green peppers (seeded and thinly sliced), and/or about 1 cup canned roasted sweet red peppers, a pot of butter or mayonnaise, and crisp rye cracker-bread. Spread cracker-bread with butter or mayonnaise. Top with bacon slices, cheese slices, and then green or red peppers.

Roast Beef Board

You can buy roast beef from a delicatessen or cook your own. Choose a 3-1/2 to 4-pound boneless roast such as crossrib or sirloin tip. Season meat with salt and cook as you like (about 1-1/2 hours for rare—130° to 135° internal temperature in a 325° oven). Serve the meat hot or cold; cold meat will not drain juices when sliced.

Place roast on a board and carve a few thin slices to get started. Pile beef between slices of pumpernickel bread (cut bread in half if you like), and embellish with butter, mustard, horseradish, chopped green onions (all served in individual containers), and cucumber to slice.

Artichoke and Salmon Tray

In a dish assemble 4 jars (6 oz. each) drained marinated artichoke hearts and about 1/2 pound thinly sliced smoked salmon or lox. Garnish with a few chopped green onions. Serve in small, split rolls (cut frozen finger rolls in half crosswise); spread bread with dill cream: Blend 1/2 teaspoon dill weed with 1 large package (8 oz.) cream cheese. Makes about 1 cup.

Fritter Buffet

SHRIMP BISQUE

CRACKERS WITH CAPERS

CHICKEN FRITTERS

VEGETABLE FRITTERS

SAUCE ROSA

GREENS WITH LEMON AND OIL DRESSING

HOT BUTTERED RYE BREAD

FIGS IMPERIAL

Fritters are an unexpected offering for a buffet party, but easily managed for smaller groups of 6 to 8. As the entrée they are served hot and crisp following a smooth shrimp bisque made from your own recipe or from canned soup. Fritters can be made several hours ahead and reheated to their original goodness.

Make the salad at the last minute using your favorite greens tossed with a simple dressing of 3 parts salad oil to 1 part fresh lemon juice, and salt and pepper to taste. Let the fig dessert decorate the buffet until time to serve.

Crackers with Capers

4   tablespoons (1/4 cup) soft butter or margarine
1   tablespoon each drained chopped capers and
    minced chives
    Unsalted crackers

Blend butter or margarine with capers and chives in a small bowl. Spread on crackers just before serving. Makes about 6 servings.

Chicken Fritters and Vegetable Fritters

3   whole chicken breasts (about 1 lb. each)
4   or 5 cups of vegetables (eggplant, cauliflower, squash,
    corn, and peas, directions follow)
    All-purpose flour
    Salt
8   eggs, beaten
    Salad oil for frying

Skin, bone and cut chicken into bite-sized chunks; cut eggplant in sticks; break cauliflower into small clusters,

cut clusters in halves or quarters; cut squash (zucchini, patty pan, or crookneck) in sticks or slices. Just before cooking the chicken and vegetable chunks, dust them in flour, sprinkle with salt, and dip in beaten egg.

To cook fritters, heat 1-1/2 inches salad oil in a deep pan to 370°; cook coated chicken and vegetable pieces a few at a time until golden brown (about 3 minutes), turning occasionally. Drain on paper toweling. Serve immediately, or place in single layer on trays lined with paper towels. Let stand up to 3 hours at room temperature, then reheat in a 375° oven for 10 to 15 minutes. Serve with Sauce Rosa (recipe follows). Makes 6 to 8 servings.

(You might prepare the vegetable fritters as small cakes as an alternative. Dice vegetables individually and with each 3/4 cup blend 1 egg, 1 tablespoon milk, 1/4 teaspoon salt, and 2 tablespoons all-purpose flour. Cook by spoonfuls as directed above.)

Sauce Rosa

1   cup (1/2 pt.) sour cream
2   tablespoons tomato paste
1/2 teaspoon paprika
1/4 teaspoon chile powder
2   teaspoons firmly packed brown sugar
1   teaspoon lemon juice

Blend sour cream with tomato paste, paprika, chile powder, brown sugar, and lemon juice in a bowl. Makes about 1 cup.

Figs Imperial

3   cups white figs or peeled black figs, cut in halves
2   tablespoons honey
1-1/2 teaspoons grated orange peel
1/2   cup orange juice
2   tablespoons lime juice
      Fig leaves
1   quart vanilla ice cream

Combine figs with honey, orange peel, orange juice, and lime juice in a saucepan. Slowly bring to a boil. Simmer 2 minutes. Remove from burner and chill fruit in syrup. Drain fruit, reserving syrup, and place decoratively on a serving dish laced with fig leaves; pour syrup in small pitcher, and serve with fruit over ice cream. Makes 6 to 8 servings.

Barbecue Buffet

BARBECUED BREAST OF CHICKEN

MADRAS FRESH FRUIT CURRY

HOT COOKED LONG GRAIN RICE

TOASTED ALMONDS   CHUTNEY

STUFFED HEARTS OF LETTUCE

FRENCH BREAD TOASTED WITH
CHIVE BUTTER

CREAM OF MINT PARFAIT

The barbecue becomes part of the buffet in this menu; the entrée comes off hot and ready to serve at once. All else is assembled and ready to go. The fruit platter is chilled, the curry sauce and rice stay hot in chafing dishes or on an electric warming tray.

Barbecued Breast of Chicken

8   large chicken breasts, split (each whole breast should be 1 lb.)
    Salt and pepper
1   cup melted butter
1-1/2   cups unsifted all-purpose flour

Rinse chicken breasts and dry meat thoroughly. Sprinkle with salt and pepper. Dip pieces, one at a time, into 3/4 cup of the melted butter, then shake in a paper bag with flour; remove and shake off excess. Place chicken on a grill 8 to 12 inches above hot coals (grill temperature should be about 375°). Cook 10 to 12 minutes on each side or until browned and meat has lost its pink color throughout (cut a gash to test). Baste during cooking with remaining melted butter. Serve immediately. Makes 8 servings.

Madras Fresh Fruit Curry

To capitalize upon temperature contrasts, top hot cooked long grain rice with cold fresh fruits, then ladle the heated curry sauce over all. Sprinkle almonds over the fruit and accompany with chutney of your choice.

On a large platter, arrange a selection of these fruits in serving pieces: pineapple wedges, cantaloupe balls, peach and pear slices (dip peach or pear slices in lemon juice), and figs or bananas (each cut into about 3 pieces and dipped in lemon juice). Cover and chill until serving. Serve with about 6 cups hot cooked long grain rice.

Curry Sauce:

2   cups dry white wine
1-1/2   cups regular strength chicken broth
2   tablespoons curry powder
1-1/2   tablespoons arrowroot (or 2 tablespoons cornstarch)
    Cold water

Combine wine and broth in a saucepan. Heat to simmering. Mix curry powder and arrowroot with enough cold water to thin to a smooth paste. Add to liquid and simmer about 5 minutes, stirring, until thickened. Serve from a chafing dish to spoon over hot rice and cold fruits. Makes 8 servings.

Stuffed Hearts of Lettuce

2   medium-sized, loosely but well-formed heads iceberg lettuce
1   cup each sour cream and mayonnaise
4   ounces crumbled blue cheese

Remove coarse outer leaves from lettuce; core. Run cold water into core to loosen leaves; drain very thoroughly. To make the dressing, whirl the sour cream, mayonnaise, and blue cheese in a blender or beat with an electric mixer until smooth. Slowly pour dressing into cored section letting it flow between leaves of lettuce heads so lettuce contains as much dressing as possible. Seal heads in clear plastic wrap. Chill 6 hours. Cut heads in quarter wedges. Serve immediately. Makes 8 servings.

Cream of Mint Parfait

1   cup hot water
1   package (3 oz.) lime-flavored gelatin
1   pint softened mint flavored ice cream
1/2   teaspoon mint extract
1   cup crushed chocolate wafer crumbs
    Whipped cream
8   mint sprigs dipped in powdered sugar

Blend hot water with flavored gelatin; stir to dissolve. Chill until cool and syrupy. With electric mixer, quickly beat ice cream and mint extract into gelatin. Sprinkle about two-thirds of the chocolate wafer crumbs in the bottom of 8 parfait glasses. Spoon in ice cream mixture. Top with remaining cooky crumbs. Refrigerate until serving time. Top each serving with a spoonful of whipped cream and a sprig of mint dipped in powdered sugar. Makes 8 servings.

A Buffet with Near Eastern Flair

KIBBEH APPETIZER   MILD ONION WEDGES

CANNED DOLMADES

DRIED OR ITALIAN OLIVES

BAKED KIBBEH   SLICED TOMATOES

ARTICHOKES WITH BREAD STUFFING

STEWED OKRA WITH ONIONS

LABNEH

CUCUMBER MINT SALAD

SWEET FRENCH BREAD

PEARS AND GRAPES

Typically, these Lebanese foods are served either cold or at room temperature; this means you can prepare everything in advance (the labneh must stand overnight). The foods are familiar to Westerners but the intriguing flavor subtleties of Lebanese cuisine come through in many of the dishes. Spread out as a buffet, this menu makes a most attractive display and is an easy way to entertain 6 to 8 people.

Basic Kibbeh

- 1   cup quick-cooking cracked wheat
    Cold water
- 1   medium-sized onion, cut up
- 2   pounds lean ground lamb
    About 1-1/2 teaspoons salt
- 1/4   teaspoon black pepper

Rinse the cracked wheat with cold water and drain. Force through the fine blade of a food chopper the onion, cracked wheat, and ground lamb. Season mixture with salt to taste and pepper; blend in 3 tablespoons cold water. Use as follows:

Kibbeh Appetizer

Measure 1 cup of the basic kibbeh, cover, and refrigerate for at least 1 hour or overnight. To serve, pat into a flat round cake, make several indentations decorat-

ively on the top of the cake with fingertips, then drizzle with about 2 teaspoons olive oil to keep surface moist. To serve, scoop kibbeh onto wedges of mild onion. Makes 6 to 8 appetizer servings.

Baked Kibbeh

Divide the balance of the basic kibbeh (minus 1 cup for the appetizer) in half and set aside while preparing the filling. In a wide frying pan, crumble 1/2 pound lean ground beef; add 2 cups finely chopped onion and 2 tablespoons olive oil. Cook, stirring, on high heat until meat is browned and onion is soft. Stir in 1/2 cup pine nuts, 1/4 teaspoon cinnamon, and salt to taste; use hot or cold.

Pat one portion of the kibbeh over the bottom of a 6 by 12-inch oval baking dish or a 9-inch square pan. Cover with the cooked beef filling; then carefully pat the remaining kibbeh over surface, making smooth. With a sharp knife cut through meat, dividing into decorative diamond shapes. Brush surface with about 2 teaspoons olive oil.

Bake kibbeh, uncovered, in a 350° oven for 30 minutes. Remove from oven and garnish with a pine nut in the center of each diamond area. Serve hot or at room temperature, cutting through at premarked divisions. Makes 6 to 8 main dish servings.

Artichokes with Bread Stuffing

- 6   to 8 artichokes, each about 3 inches in diameter
    Vinegar
    Water
- 1/2   cup fine dry bread crumbs
- 1/2   cup finely chopped parsley
- 1/2   teaspoon oregano
- 1/2   teaspoon salt
- 6   tablespoons olive oil

Cut off the top two-thirds of each artichoke, then break off coarse outer bracts down to the pale inner bracts that are completely edible. Trim green exterior from base and cut so artichokes will sit on stem end. Gently pry open inner bracts of each artichoke and with a spoon scoop out and discard the fuzzy choke. Drop artichokes in acid-water (1 tablespoon vinegar for each 1 quart water) as prepared.

In a frying pan, combine bread crumbs, parsley, oregano, salt, and 4 tablespoons of the olive oil. Cook, stirring, until bread is toasted but not scorched.

Drain artichokes; then pat bread mixture firmly onto cut tops of artichokes, forcing crumbs down into the center. Set artichokes side by side, crumbs up, in a large pan containing 1/2-inch water and 1 tablespoon vinegar. Cover pan, bring to a boil, then reduce to a simmer, and cook gently for 15 minutes or until artichokes pierce easily; add a little water if needed. Lift artichokes from pan and let cool to room temperature. Drizzle with a mixture of the remaining 2 tablespoons olive oil and 1 tablespoon vinegar. Makes 6 to 8 servings.

Stewed Okra with Onions

    1   package (10 oz.) frozen okra, thawed
        Boiling water
    6   to 8 small boiling onions
    2   tablespoons olive oil
    4   tablespoons water
  1/2   cup finely chopped fresh coriander, or 1/2 cup finely
        chopped parsley and 1/2 teaspoon whole coriander
        seed
    1   small clove garlic, minced
    2   tablespoons lemon juice

Drop thawed okra into boiling water to cover and cook 2 to 3 minutes or just until okra is easy to pierce. (Use fresh okra if in season. Trim stem ends from 1/2 to 2/3 pound. Cook in boiling water to cover for 5 minutes.) Drain okra at once and immerse in ice water to cool quickly. When cold, drain and set aside.

Peel onions and place in a medium-sized frying pan with olive oil and water. Cover and cook over moderately low heat until water evaporates, then continue cooking, turning onions occasionally until they are lightly browned; browning takes about 10 minutes.

Uncover pan and add coriander and garlic. Add okra and cook, stirring, until okra is warm. Place in a serving dish and serve hot or at room temperature. Just before serving, drizzle lemon juice over the vegetables. Makes 6 to 8 servings.

Labneh (yogurt cheese)

Line a colander with a muslin cloth; pour in 1 quart unflavored yogurt. Bring cloth together over yogurt, twisting ends lightly together to enclose the yogurt. Place colander in a larger bowl and let drain for at least 24 hours. Scoop labneh from cloth and place in a bowl; salt to taste. Cover labneh and refrigerate until ready to serve; it keeps at least a week. Makes about 2 cups.

Cucumber Mint Salad

    1   large cucumber, peeled and thinly sliced
    1   cup unflavored yogurt
    1   tablespoon minced fresh mint leaves or 1 tablespoon
        crumbled dried mint
        Salt to taste

Mix cucumber slices with yogurt, mint, and salt. Serve cold. Makes 6 to 8 servings.

Pirog Buffet

LAMB AND MUSHROOM PIROG

VEGETABLE SALAD TRAY

ORANGE CHIFFON SOUFFLÉ

A pirog is a big meat filled pastry; this one is of Russian origin. Although somewhat involved to make, it is quite a spectacular offering and can be made the day before.

The tray salad is an attractive way to present vegetables and dressing separately so that they remain fresh and appetizing for leisurely buffet service. The dessert is another item made ahead and comes from the refrigerator.

Lamb and Mushroom Pirog

  1/2   cup warm water (lukewarm for compressed yeast)
    1   package yeast, active dry or compressed
  1/2   teaspoon salt
    2   teaspoons sugar
    3   eggs
  1/2   cup (1/4 lb.) soft butter
3-1/2   cups regular all-purpose flour, unsifted
        Salad oil
        Lamb and mushroom filling (directions follow),
        chilled
    1   egg yolk beaten with 1 tablespoon water

Measure water into a large bowl and stir in the yeast. Let stand about 5 minutes and stir in salt, sugar, and eggs. Cut butter in small pieces and add to liquid. Add the flour and mix with a heavy spoon until moistened. Shape into a compact ball with your hands and place on a floured board. Knead until smooth and elastic, about 5 minutes. Rinse mixing bowl, dry it, and coat with salad oil. Place dough in bowl and turn over once to oil surface. Cover and let rise in a warm place until dough is about double in volume (it takes about an hour).

Knead dough on a lightly floured board to remove air bubbles. Pinch off a portion about 1/2-cup size and set aside. Shape the large lump of dough into a smooth ball. Lightly flour a pastry cloth and roll ball of dough out on it to a rectangle 10 by 18 inches. Spoon cold lamb and mushroom filling onto half of the dough toward one end. Shape filling with hands into a compact rectangle, leaving about 1-1/2-inch margin on the three outside edges. Using cloth to guide, lift the exposed section of dough over the filling. Neatly lap bottom edge up over the sides and pinch firmly around top rim.

Place a greased rimless baking sheet, top side down, on the pirog. Supporting with the pastry cloth and pan, invert pirog onto baking sheet.

Roll reserved dough into a rectangle about 3 or 4 inches by 12 inches and cut in 1/2-inch-wide strips, 12 inches long.

Arrange dough strips decoratively over the top of the pirog, tucking the ends of dough beneath the pirog with fingers or tip of a knife.

Let rise in a warm place for about 20 minutes. Brush exposed surfaces with egg-water mixture. Prick top of dough in 6 to 8 places with a fork. Bake in a 350° oven for 50 minutes, or until dough is richly browned. Serve pirog hot, cut in rectangles.

To bake ahead, cool hot pirog thoroughly on a wire rack. Wrap and chill as long as 24 hours. Place cold, unwrapped pirog on an ungreased baking sheet, cover loosely with foil, and bake in a 350° oven for 50 minutes. Makes 6 to 8 servings.

Lamb and Mushroom Filling:

Melt 3 tablespoons butter or margarine in a Dutch oven. Add 2 pounds thinly sliced mushrooms, mix with butter, cover, and cook over medium heat for about 5 minutes to draw out juices; stir occasionally.

Remove cover and turn heat high and cook, stirring frequently, for about 10 minutes or until all liquid is gone. Mix in 2 tablespoons flour, 2 teaspoons dill weed, and 1/2 cup sour cream; cook, stirring, until bubbling and blended. Pour mushroom mixture into a large bowl and set aside.

Rinse frying pan, and add 1-1/2 pounds ground lamb. Cook over high heat, stirring and breaking up meat, until richly browned. Skim off and discard fat. Stir lamb into mushroom mixture, add 3/4 teaspoon salt or to taste, cover, and chill thoroughly.

Vegetable Salad Tray

About 2 cups thinly sliced romaine lettuce
About 2 cups (2 bunches) radishes, thinly sliced
1   medium-sized cucumber, thinly sliced
About 1 cup thinly sliced green onions (6 to 8) including several inches of the tops
2   to 3 large tomatoes, peeled and cut in wedges
1   cup (8 oz.) diced feta cheese (optional)
Herb dressing (recipe follows)

On a large rimmed tray arrange separately the lettuce, radishes, cucumber, green onions, and tomatoes. Place cheese in a small bowl. To make ahead, cover salad and cheese with clear plastic film and refrigerate up to 5 hours. To serve, spoon the cheese and the herb dressing onto individual portions. Makes 8 to 10 servings.

Herb Dressing:

3   tablespoons minced fresh parsley
1-1/2   tablespoons minced fresh mint (or 1-1/2 tablespoons dry mint, crushed)
1   clove garlic, minced
1   tablespoon dill weed
3/4   teaspoon salt
1/4   teaspoon pepper
1/2   teaspoon sugar
6   tablespoons lemon juice
1/3   cup red wine vinegar
3/4   cup olive oil or salad oil

Combine in a bowl parsley, mint, garlic. Blend with dill weed, salt, pepper, sugar, lemon juice, red wine vinegar, and oil; do not refrigerate. Blend dressing before serving and pour into a small serving bowl.

Orange Chiffon Soufflé

2   envelopes unflavored gelatin
1   cup sugar
    Dash salt
2   cups cold water
6   eggs, separated
2   cans (6 oz. each) frozen orange juice concentrate, thawed
1/4   cup lemon juice
1/2   teaspoon each grated orange peel and lemon peel
1/3   cup toasted slivered almonds
    Whole strawberries (optional)
    Soft custard sauce (recipe follows)

Mix gelatin, 3/4 cup of the sugar, and salt in the top of a double boiler; stir in water and heat until gelatin dissolves. Beat egg yolks until light and stir in the gelatin mixture. Return to the double boiler, place over a pan of hot water, and cook, stirring, until mixture coats the spoon in an even layer. Remove from heat and stir in orange concentrate, lemon juice, and grated citrus peels. Chill until it just starts to congeal.

Beat egg whites until soft peaks form and gradually beat in the remaining 1/4 cup sugar. Fold meringue into the syrupy chilled orange mixture. Fold a 20-inch length of waxed paper into thirds lengthwise and secure with paper clips around a 2-quart soufflé dish to form a collar. Spoon in soufflé mixture. Chill until set.

When ready to serve, carefully remove paper strip and press the almonds around rim of soufflé. Garnish with strawberries. Serve with chilled custard sauce. Makes 10 to 12 servings.

Soft Custard Sauce:

Scald 2 cups milk in the top of a double boiler. Mix 1/3 cup sugar and 1 tablespoon cornstarch and blend in the hot milk; return to the top of the double boiler, and, stirring constantly, cook until thickened. Beat 3 egg yolks to blend. Mix with some of the hot sauce, then return all to pan. Cook, stirring, until slightly thickened. Stir in 1 teaspoon vanilla. Cool, then chill.

Lasagne Buffet

LASAGNE NAPOLI

TOSSED GREEN SALAD WITH SALTED NUTS

GARLIC FRENCH DRESSING

HOT BUTTERED CRUSTY ROLLS

GRAHAM RIBBON LOAF

HOT APPLE CIDER

This is a good choice for an after-the-game supper. The lasagne can be assembled the day before, refrigerated, then baked before serving. The dessert should be made ahead and refrigerated overnight. So you only have to bake the lasagne, warm the rolls, and mix the salad at serving time. Serve mugs of hot apple cider with the dessert loaf.

Lasagne Napoli

1   medium-sized onion, chopped
1   clove garlic, minced or mashed
2   tablespoons olive oil or salad oil
1   pound lean ground beef
1   can (3 or 4 oz.) sliced mushrooms
1   can (8 oz.) tomato sauce
1   can (6 oz.) tomato paste
2   teaspoons salt
1   teaspoon crumbled oregano
3/4 cup water
2   eggs
1   package (10 oz.) frozen chopped spinach, thawed
1   cup cream-style cottage cheese
1/3 cup grated Parmesan cheese
    Lasagne (12 oz.), cooked and drained
1   package (8 oz.) process American cheese slices cut in strips

In a medium-sized frying pan, lightly brown onion and garlic in 1 tablespoon of the oil; add ground beef,

and break apart; cook until brown. Blend in mushrooms (including mushroom liquid), tomato sauce, tomato paste, 1 teaspoon of the salt, oregano, and water; simmer 15 minutes. Meanwhile, mix 1 of the eggs with the spinach, cottage cheese, Parmesan cheese, remaining 1 tablespoon oil, and 1 teaspoon salt. Beat the second egg slightly and stir into the cooked lasagne. Pour half the meat sauce into an oblong baking pan (about 9 by 13 inches) and cover with a layer of half the lasagne. Spread all the spinach mixture over lasagne. Complete layers with remaining lasagne and meat sauce. (Refrigerate at this point, if desired.) Cover and bake in a 350° oven for 45 minutes; (if refrigerated, bake 1 hour). Remove cover and arrange strips of American cheese on top; bake for 15 minutes longer. Serve hot. Makes 6 to 8 servings.

Tossed Green Salad with Salted Nuts

Just before serving, mix crisp salad greens (1 cup for each serving) lightly with garlic French dressing (1 tablespoon for each serving) and sprinkle with a handful of coarsely chopped salted peanuts or mixed nuts.

Graham Ribbon Loaf

2   cups whipping cream
2   tablespoons sugar
2   tablespoons cocoa
24 square regular or cinnamon graham crackers
2   or 3 tablespoons toasted flaked coconut

Whip cream with sugar and cocoa. Spread a layer of cream about 1/4 inch thick on one side of each graham cracker. Stand them on edge on a serving plate, with layers of cream between crackers, so that they form a loaf shape—you should use about half of the whipped cream mixture. Coat top and sides of loaf with remaining cream; sprinkle top with toasted coconut. Cover loosely and refrigerate overnight. For a ribbon effect, cut slices on a diagonal. Makes 8 servings.

Foreign Themes

A unique way to entertain is to have a party with an international theme. The authentic foreign menus in this chapter are adapted to our foods and customs. Some may be more familiar than others, such as the Greek dinner with Shish kebabs, Arab bread, and Baklava. Others may not be as familiar such as the North African Couscous which is a complete one-dish-meal.

Try using serving techniques native to a particular country to add to the charm of your party. Stage the Swiss Raclette party in front of a blazing fireplace; the fire adds not only atmosphere but actually cooks the entrée. To serve the Mandarin brunch group, seat the guests around small tables and invite them to help themselves to a choice of pancake fillings.

Specific shopping directions are included in each menu when unusual ingredients are required; however, readily available alternates are also suggested.

Stage a dinner party based on a foreign theme. Here a Mexican dinner is being casually prepared and leisurely served on the patio. Guests contribute to the mood by wearing casual or native costumes. A Mexican fiesta can be found on page 48.

A Mexican Fiesta

GUACAMOLE WITH POMEGRANATE SEEDS

TOSTADAS (TOASTED TORTILLA WEDGES)

MOLE DE GUAJOLOTE   SOPAIPILLAS

RICE   GREEN SALAD

BAKED PINEAPPLE, NATILLAS

Music is the touch that turns this or any Mexican party into a fiesta. Round up your own mariachis or settle for records. Bright and gay decorations such as a piñata add to the special mood.

Guacamole with Pomegranate Seeds

3   large ripe avocados
1   clove garlic, mashed
1   can (4 oz.) whole California green chiles, chopped (optional)
    About 3 tablespoons lemon juice
    About 1 teaspoon salt
    Cayenne and lemon juice to taste
    Pomegranate seeds
    Tostadas (see below)

Mash avocados with a fork until almost smooth, with some definite chunks showing. Add garlic, chiles (if desired), lemon juice, salt, and cayenne. Place in a bowl and sprinkle top with pomegranate seeds. Scoop onto tostadas to eat. Makes 8 to 12 servings.

Tostadas

A tostada is any toasted corn tortilla, garnished or not. Cut 8 to 12 tortillas in six pie-shaped wedges, and fry a few at a time in about 1 inch salad oil heated to 370° until crisp and brown; takes a few seconds. Drain on absorbent material, store air tight until ready to serve. Makes 8 to 12 servings.

Mole de Guajolote

This simplified version of the classic Mexican dish is a blend of a multitude of flavors—but instead of using the several varieties of chiles as is traditional, here you use a quantity of chile powder. You can prepare the mole early in the day or start the day before by cooking the turkey; reheat to serve.

1/2   cup unsifted all-purpose flour
      About 1 tablespoon salt
      12-pound turkey, disjointed or 4 pounds turkey breasts and 3 pounds turkey thighs (including giblets)
      About 1/2 cup lard or shortening
      Water
2   large or 3 medium-size onions, chopped
1   large clove garlic, chopped
1/2   cup seedless raisins
2   ounces unsweetened chocolate, chopped
1/4   teaspoon each ground anise, coriander, cumin, and cloves
1/2   cup peanut butter
1   can (8 oz.) tomato sauce
      About 3/4 cup chile powder
2   toasted bread slices, broken in coarse crumbs
4   corn tortillas
2   tablespoons sesame seeds
1   tablespoon sugar
10   cups hot cooked rice

Blend flour and 1 teaspoon of the salt and rub evenly onto turkey pieces. Brown pieces in 1/2 cup lard in a wide frying pan over medium heat. Put turkey in a large kettle, just barely covered with water, add 2 teaspoons of the salt; cover and simmer until tender to pierce. Cool in broth; lift out turkey, remove bones, and cut meat in large serving pieces. Cover and chill meat. Return bones to broth, adding neck, gizzard, wing tips, and simmer until reduced to 6 cups; pour broth through a wire strainer and discard bones. Chill until ready to use.

To make sauce: Add onions to pan in which you browned the turkey, and cook, stirring, until lightly browned; add more lard if necessary. Add garlic, raisins, chocolate, anise, coriander, cumin, cloves, peanut butter, tomato sauce, chile powder, and toast; heat through, stirring, and set aside.

Rub surfaces of corn tortillas with water and toast, one at a time, in a dry frying pan over medium heat, turning frequently until they begin to harden. Break in chunks and add to the sauce mixture. Place sesame seed in the same dry frying pan and stir over medium heat until golden and lightly toasted; add to sauce.

Whirl sauce in a blender (a portion at a time) until smooth, using 2 cups of the reserved turkey broth for liquid. (If you don't have a blender, grind the raisins, bread, and tortillas; mix with the other ingredients; and force through wire strainer or food mill.) Add the remaining 4 cups turkey broth and the sugar. Pour through a wire strainer and add more salt or chile powder to taste.

Add turkey meat to the mole sauce, heat slowly on top of the range and serve with rice. Makes 10 to 12 servings.

Sopaipillas

    4   cups sifted all-purpose flour
1-1/4   teaspoons salt
    1   tablespoon baking powder
    3   tablespoons sugar
    2   tablespoons shortening
         About 1-1/4 cups milk
         Salad oil for frying
         Butter

Stir flour to blend with salt, baking powder, and sugar; rub in shortening with fingers until particles are all of even texture. Stir in enough milk to make a soft dough just firm enough to roll. Allow dough to stand for 30 to 60 minutes, then on a lightly floured board roll 1/4 inch thick and cut in diamond-shaped pieces. Fry in 1-1/2 inches salad oil heated to 390° to 400°. Turn at once so they will puff evenly, then turn back to brown both sides. Drain on absorbent material. Serve hot or cold with butter, as a bread. Store air-tight. Makes about 4 dozen.

Baked Pineapple, Natillas

    2   medium-sized fresh ripe pineapples
1/4   cup sugar
    2   or 3 tablespoons rum or 1 teaspoon rum flavoring
    4   tablespoons (1/4 cup) butter
         Natillas (recipe follows)

Lay each pineapple on its side and cut off a thick slice that does not include the green top. Carefully scoop out the insides of the shell using a grapefruit knife and cut pineapple meat into bite-sized pieces. Sweeten with sugar, and blend in rum. Put pineapple pieces back into pineapple shells. Dot the top with butter, cover with foil (including the leaves), and bake in a 350° oven for 40 minutes. Replace the top and bring it to the table on a plate to serve warm, into desert bowls; ladle Natillas sauce over fruit.

Natillas:

1/4   teaspoon salt
1/4   cup sugar
    2   teaspoons cornstarch
    2   cups (1 pt.) half-and-half
    1   egg
    2   egg yolks
    1   teaspoon vanilla

Mix salt, sugar and cornstarch in the top of a double boiler. Blend in cream and cook over boiling water, stirring, for 10 minutes or until thickened. Beat egg and egg yolks to blend and mix with a little of the hot mixture; then return all to double boiler and cook, stirring, over simmering water, until slightly thickened. Add vanilla. Chill, covered.

Greek Barbecue Party

ASSORTED APPETIZERS: ROASTED PUMPKIN
SEEDS, OLIVES, ALMONDS

BARBECUED SHISH KEBAB

MINTED GREEN SALAD   CUMIN RICE

ARAB BREAD OR SWEET FRENCH BREAD

CRENSHAW MELON WEDGES   BAKLAVA

The roasted pumpkin seeds can be found in the gourmet sections of a supermarket. Start with a whole leg of lamb to make shish kebab for 6 to 8 servings; marinate it a day in advance.

The Arab bread can be made days ahead and frozen, but if you prefer you can buy the bread, as well as the baklava, in a store that specializes in Middle Eastern foods.

The salad and rice can be made with ease just before serving. If you serve out-of-doors or buffet style, keep the rice warm in a covered casserole.

The baklava tastes fresher if you reheat it before serving. Place pieces slightly apart on a baking pan, uncovered, and heat in a 325° oven for 15 minutes.

Barbecued Shish Kebab

    6   to 7 pound leg of lamb, boned
         Marinade (recipe follows)
    2   large green peppers
    1   large white onion

Cut lamb into 1-1/2-inch cubes and place in a bowl. Pour in marinade and mix, cover, and chill overnight, stirring meat several times.

Cut the peppers into eighths, making approximately 1-1/2-inch pieces, discarding seeds. Cut onion into eighths. Alternate on each of 8 skewers about 4 or 5 lamb cubes, 2 pieces green pepper, and 1 piece onion. Barbecue about 6 inches over hot coals, basting often with marinade and turning to brown on all sides, allowing about 15 minutes for medium-rare meat. Makes 8 servings.

Marinade:

Mix 1/2 cup dry Sherry (or apple juice) with 1/4 cup olive oil, 2 teaspoons *each* salt and oregano, 1/2 teaspoon pepper, and 1 large onion, thinly sliced.

Minted Green Salad

3	tablespoons lemon juice
1/2	cup olive oil
1	teaspoon each salt and crushed dried mint
1/2	teaspoon pepper
2	quarts bite-sized pieces mixed salad greens
1	cup cherry tomatoes, halved
1/2	cup sliced ripe olives

Blend lemon juice, olive oil, salt, mint, and pepper at least 1 hour. Combine in a serving bowl the greens, tomatoes, olives, and dressing; mix well and serve at once. Makes 6 to 8 servings.

Cumin Rice

4-1/2	tablespoons butter or margarine
1-1/2	cups long grain rice
1-1/2	teaspoons salt
1	tablespoon ground cumin
4	cups boiling water
1/2	cup pine nuts

Melt 1-1/2 tablespoons of the butter or margarine in a saucepan, add rice and stir until rice is golden brown. Add salt, cumin, and boiling water. Cover and simmer 25 minutes, or until rice is fluffy and moisture is absorbed. Spoon into a serving dish. Melt the remaining 3 tablespoons butter or margarine, add pine nuts, and sauté, shaking pan, until nuts are golden brown. Spoon over hot rice. Makes 6 to 8 servings.

Arab Bread

There are two important directions that must be carefully followed when making this chewy flat bun. The first essential thing is to roll the dough to a precise and even thickness and let the rounds rise exactly as directed. The second essential thing is to preheat the oven for at least 30 minutes before the start of baking and check the temperature with a mercury oven thermometer for an even, hot baking temperature.

2-1/2	cups warm water (about 110°)
2	packages active dry yeast
1/4	teaspoon sugar
6	cups regular sifted all-purpose flour
1-1/2	teaspoons salt
3	tablespoons olive oil or salad oil

Pour 1/2 cup of the water into a small bowl, add yeast and sugar, and stir until dissolved. Place flour, salt, and oil in a large bowl; add the yeast mixture and the remaining 2 cups water and beat with a wooden spoon or a heavy duty electric mixer until the flour is completely moistened. Turn out on a floured board; knead until smooth, satiny, and no longer sticky, about 10 minutes. Place in a bowl, grease the top lightly, cover, and let rise in a warm place until doubled in size, about 1-1/2 hours.

Turn out on a lightly floured board and knead lightly to remove air bubbles. Roll into a log 16 inches long; then cut into 16 equal pieces. Pat each piece of dough into a ball; then use a rolling pin on a floured board to roll each ball into a circle 6-1/2 inches in diameter and 3/16 inch thick (precise thickness is important but the circle may be irregular). Place each round on 6-1/2-inch squares of ungreased foil. Let stand uncovered for 1 hour. (Do not place in a warm spot to hurry the rising.)

Meanwhile place oven rack at the lowest point and preheat oven to 500°. Place 4 breads at a time, still on foil, directly on the oven rack. Bake about 5 minutes, or until puffed and just starting to brown. Remove from oven and either serve at once with butter or slip into plastic bags while still warm to keep the bread moist and pliable. Let cool and freeze. To reheat Arab bread, stack 4 to 6 rounds and seal in foil. Reheat in a 375° oven for 10 to 15 minutes, or until hot through. Makes 16 individual serving size loaves, 6-1/2 inches in diameter.

North African Couscous

COUSCOUS

FRESH FRUIT PLATTER

TEA

This dish native to North Africa is a complete meal in itself. Guests help themselves from the mound of steamed wheat in the middle of a large serving platter and add portions of the surrounding meats and vegetables. Then they spoon on garbanzos, pour hot cooking broth over all and add a few judicious drops of hot sauce. The dish in its entirety is called couscous (*koos-koos*) but it is the hard wheat pellet, itself, that is actually the couscous. It is available in specialty stores.

Couscous

    2   tablespoons olive oil or salad oil
    3   each chicken legs and thighs, cut apart
1-1/2   pounds boneless lamb stew meat, cut in
        1-1/2-inch cubes
    1   medium-sized onion, chopped
    5   medium-sized carrots, peeled and cut in 1-inch
        pieces
  1/4   teaspoon pepper
    1   large can (about 48 oz.) chicken broth
    1   can (about 9 oz.) garbanzos, drained
        Hot sauce (recipe follows)
1-1/2   cups couscous or quick-cooking cracked wheat
        (also called bulgur or kasha)
    6   tablespoons butter or margarine
    3   stalks celery, cut in 1-inch pieces
    1   green pepper, seeded and cut in strips
    1   can (14 oz.) artichoke hearts in water, drained

Heat olive oil in a Dutch oven over medium heat. Sauté chicken legs and thighs until brown; remove to bowl. Add lamb and brown, stirring; remove to bowl with chicken. Add onion and stir until golden. Return chicken and lamb to pan and add carrots, pepper, and 4 cups of the broth. Reduce heat, cover, and simmer for 40 minutes or until chicken is tender.

Meanwhile remove garbanzos to serving bowl and prepare hot sauce (recipe follows). Then prepare couscous or bulgur wheat according to directions on the package using remaining chicken broth as part of the liquid called for. When cooked, remove from heat and, with a fork, gently break grains apart using a tossing motion. Add butter in chunks and continue tossing with fork until grains are coated. Cover and set aside to keep warm.

When meats have simmered 40 minutes, add celery and pepper and simmer 5 minutes more. Then add artichoke hearts and remove from heat. Strain broth from vegetables into a bowl, skim off excess fat, and pour into a teapot or pitcher for serving.

Mound couscous in center of a large platter. Arrange meat and vegetables attractively around side and serve immediately with bowls of hot sauce, garbanzos, and broth.

Hot Sauce:

    2   teaspoons catsup
    1   teaspoon olive oil
  1/4   teaspoon each cayenne, ground cumin,
        and white pepper
  1/8   teaspoon each ground nutmeg and ground cloves
    2   tablespoons hot broth from vegetable and meat
        mixture

Blend the catsup and olive oil. Then stir in cayenne, cumin, white pepper, nutmeg, and cloves. Just before serving blend in the hot broth.

A Roman Feast

MELON WITH PROSCIUTTO

BREAD STICKS

SCALOPPINE DI TACCHINO

(TURKEY SCALOPPINE)

ASPARACI (ASPARAGUS WITH HOLLANDAISE)

PATATE FRITTI (POTATO PUFFS)

SWEET FRENCH ROLLS   BUTTER

INSALATA ROMANA (ROMAINE SALAD)

CASSATA DI FRAGOLE (STRAWBERRY
MERINGUE CAKE)

ASSORTED FRESH FRUITS

A menu highlighting the elegant foods of Rome makes an excellent choice for a gourmet dinner party. Serve it in courses in keeping with European fashion. Have melon on the table when your guests sit down. For the main course, bring serving dishes filled with turkey, asparagus, and potatoes to the table along with warm dinner plates. A California wine that an Italian might choose would be Sylvaner. Offer it with the entrée. The salad course follows and is to be served onto chilled plates at the table. Present the whole cassata to cut and serve; an excellent choice for a beverage is chilled sweet champagne.

Provide each guest with a fruit plate, knife, and finger bowl; pass the platter of fruits. It will be a production your friends won't soon forget.

Melon with Prosciutto

Prosciutto (Italian ham), sliced paper thin, is available in many markets or at Italian delicatessens. You will need about 1/4 pound for 6 servings.

Cut a ripe cantaloupe into 6 wedges. Remove seeds. Cut melon from rind except at ends and then slice crosswise into bite-sized pieces. Drape a strip of prosciutto over the top of each melon wedge. Garnish each plate with one or two black olives and lemon wedge. Offer black pepper in a mill for each person to grind over his fruit.

Scaloppine di Tacchino

Tender pieces of boned turkey breast are cooked here in a flavorful Marsala wine sauce; this can be done ahead, then reheat and finish the dish with a satiny egg and cream glaze. Half of a whole breast from a 13-pound hen will make 6 servings; if you must purchase a whole breast, freeze one section for another meal.

1/2   of a whole breast from a 13- to 14-pound turkey hen (about 3 pounds)
      All-purpose flour, salt, and pepper
1/2   cup olive oil
1/2   cup (1/4 lb.) butter
  1   cup Marsala wine
1/4   teaspoon crushed oregano
1/2   pound mushrooms, sliced
1/2   can (10-1/2 oz. size) condensed consommé
  1   egg yolk
  1   tablespoon whipping cream

Skin and bone turkey; slice meat across grain as thinly as possible. Coat slices in flour seasoned with salt and pepper; shake off excess. In a large frying pan, heat olive oil and 1/4 cup of the butter over medium heat. Lightly brown turkey slices on both sides, a few at a time; pour out fat and return meat to frying pan with Marsala wine and oregano. Cook, uncovered, over medium heat until liquid is almost evaporated (about 8 minutes), turning meat gently to cook evenly on all sides. Sauté mushrooms in the second 1/4 cup butter and cook until limp and liquid is evaporated, stirring; add mushrooms and butter to turkey. Add consommé. (At this point you can cover and chill the turkey.) Cook turkey mixture at simmer until almost dry; 10 to 15 minutes on low heat. Beat egg yolk with cream; remove turkey from heat. Pour the mixture over meat; turn meat gently to glaze all sides. Serve immediately. Makes 6 servings.

Asparaci

In a wide frying pan, uncovered, cook 2-1/2 pounds trimmed asparagus in boiling salted water to cover just until tender. Drain, and arrange in serving dish. Pass Hollandaise Sauce (recipe follows) or use 1 to 1-1/2 cups canned hollandaise sauce. Ladle over asparagus. Makes 6 servings.

Hollandaise Sauce:

    3   egg yolks
1-1/2   tablespoons lemon juice
    1   tablespoon water
        Dash cayenne
    1   teaspoon Dijon-style mustard
    1   cup hot melted butter

Combine yolks, lemon juice, water, cayenne, and mustard in a blender. Cover and whirl to blend. With motor at high speed, remove lid and gradually pour in butter, increasing flow of butter as sauce thickens. Turn off motor at once. Serve, or chill and reheat, stirring, over a pan of hot water. Makes about 1-1/4 cups.

Patate Fritti

These fragile, moist potatoes are a combination of cream puff paste and soft mashed potatoes. They can be eaten immediately after frying, or wrapped in foil and reheated in the oven.

    1/2   cup hot water
      4   tablespoons (1/4 cup) butter
    1/8   teaspoon salt
    1/2   cup sifted all-purpose flour
      2   eggs
  1-1/2   cups hot mashed potatoes
      3   tablespoons grated Parmesan cheese
          Salt and pepper to taste
          Salad oil

Bring water, butter, and salt to a boil; add the 1/2 cup flour all at once, and beat over low heat until mixture leaves sides of pan and forms a compact ball. Remove from heat; continue beating to cool mixture slightly, about 2 minutes. Add eggs, one at a time, beating well after each addition; continue beating until mixture has a satin-like sheen.

Combine mashed potatoes with the hot cooked mixture and Parmesan cheese; season to taste with salt and pepper. Cool. Roll spoonfuls of dough on a lightly floured board to shape cylinders or cones about 1 by 2-1/2 inches. In a heavy frying pan heat salad oil (about 3/4 inch deep) to 370°. Lightly brown potatoes on all sides; drain on paper towels. Serve hot or reheat; to

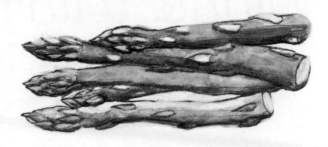

reheat, wrap in foil and place in a 350° oven for 25 minutes. Makes 12 puffs.

Insalata Romana

In a salad bowl rubbed with a cut clove garlic, mix 4 to 6 cups broken romaine leaves with 1/3 to 1/2 cup dressing made of 3 parts olive oil to 1 part wine vinegar. Season with salt and freshly ground black pepper. Makes 6 servings.

Cassata di Fragole

      6   egg whites
  1-1/2   cups sugar
      1   teaspoon vinegar
          Strawberry cream filling (recipe follows)
          Whole strawberries with stems for garnish

In large bowl of electric mixer, beat egg whites until foamy. Gradually add sugar 1 tablespoon at a time, beating until sugar is completely dissolved and soft peaks form. Beat in vinegar. Turn into a well-greased 9-inch cheese cake pan with removable bottom or spring released sides; spread smooth on top. Bake in a 325° oven for 1 hour. Place on wire rack to cool thoroughly. (Center of meringue will drop.) When meringue is thoroughly cool, slip a slender knife around edge to release. Remove sides of pan. Fill center of meringue with strawberry cream filling. (If edges of meringue break off, replace, securing with filling.) Serve immediately or chill lightly covered in refrigerator as long as overnight. Before serving, decorate cake top with strawberries. Cut into wedges to serve. Makes 10 to 12 servings.

Strawberry Cream Filling:

    2   cups strawberries
  1/3   cup sugar
    2   cups (1 pt.) whipping cream
    1   teaspoon vanilla

Hull and slice strawberries. Mix gently with sugar. Whip cream with vanilla until stiff. Fold in sliced strawberries. Use at once.

Dinner with International Flavor

This menu selects from the cuisines of various nationalities to become a harmonious whole. Prepare the salad early in the day and allow it to marinate. You can also make the pie ahead of time and chill; sprinkle on toffee topping just before serving.

California Consommé

Heat 3 cans (10-1/2 oz. *each*) condensed consommé. Add 1/4 cup dry Sherry and garnish each serving with 1 or 2 diced artichoke bottoms (cooked fresh or frozen, or canned). Makes 6 servings.

Swedish Sesame Crisps

Brush wafer-thin pieces of Swedish *flatbröd* with melted butter, sprinkle with sesame seeds, and broil until toasted lightly.

French Coq au Vin

3	to 4-pound broiler fryer chicken, cut in serving-sized pieces
2	tablespoons all-purpose flour
1	small onion, chopped
3	tablespoons olive oil
3	cups each dry red wine and regular strength chicken broth
	Herb bouquet of 1 bay leaf, 4 parsley sprigs, 2 sprigs marjoram or thyme (or 1/4 teaspoon dried marjoram or thyme)
1	clove garlic
18	small onions (about 1 pound), peeled
1/2	pound whole, small mushrooms with stems trimmed
1/2	teaspoon salt
	Buttered, toasted French bread slices

Coat chicken with flour shaking off excess. In a heavy kettle, cook chopped onion in oil until soft; add chicken and brown well on all sides. Pour in wine and broth; add herb bouquet and garlic (impale garlic on a wooden pick). Add whole onions, mushrooms, and salt. Cover kettle and simmer for 30 to 45 minutes, or until meat is tender when pierced. Remove and discard garlic. Serve garnished with toasted French bread. Makes 6 servings.

Gold and Green Mediterranean Salad

1-1/2	pounds carrots, peeled
1-1/2	cups finely minced parsley
1	cup olive oil or salad oil
6	tablespoons vinegar
1/8	teaspoon thyme
	Freshly ground black pepper
1-1/2	teaspoons salt
	Lettuce leaves

Slice carrots as thin as possible; this may be done with vegetable peeler, cutting on the diagonal. Cook carrots in boiling water to cover for 2 minutes. Drain carrots and pour over them a mixture of parsley, olive oil or salad oil, vinegar, thyme, pepper, and salt. Cover and chill at least 2 hours. Serve carrots with dressing on leaves of lettuce. Makes 6 servings.

English Toffee Pie

4	egg yolks
1/3	cup sugar
1/8	teaspoon salt
2	teaspoons unflavored gelatin
2	tablespoons cold water
1/2	pint (1 cup) whipping cream
2	tablespoons rum or rum flavoring to taste
1	baked 9-inch pie shell
1/4	pound English toffee candy, chopped coarsely

Beat egg yolks until light and thick; add sugar and salt. Soften gelatin in cold water and dissolve over hot water. Mix well with yolks. Whip cream until stiff, combine with egg mixture and rum, and pour into a baked pie shell. Chill until set. Before serving, sprinkle toffee over top of pie. Makes 6 servings.

Swiss Peasant Dinner
. . . . . . Raclette

RACLETTE

TINY BOILED POTATOES

MARINATED ONIONS AND PICKLES

GREEN SALAD

WINTER PEARS   ALMONDS IN SHELLS

The fireplace is the setting for this leisurely party. It is based on the Swiss dish *raclette* (from the French *racler*, to scrape). Push a hunk of cheese close to the fire until it begins to melt on the surface; scrape off this golden cream and spoon at once onto hot boiled potatoes (or slices of crusty bread).

Gather a small group around the fire and work your way through raclette with Pinot Chardonnay, Barbera, or Zinfandel to refresh the palate; salad can go with the raclette or follow it. Pears, nuts, and a rich red Port on display during the early part of the meal become the climax.

Raclette

For dramatic effect a chunk of cheese at least 2 to 3 pounds is best, although any size will work. The cheese intended for this dish is the Swiss-made raclette. More common cheeses with mellow flavors that melt smoothly are also ideal: Gruyère, fontina, Samsoe, and Swiss. Avoid cheeses that string such as mozzarella.

Place cheese, trimmed of any wax, in an attractive, large shallow pan. Set pan on the hearth and push the wide surface of the cheese in close to the fire. When the cheese face begins to melt, scrape it off and spoon onto a bite of hot potato and eat with marinated onions (directions follow) and sweet pickles. Crusty French bread slices can be served as an alternate for the potatoes.

Pull cheese away from the heat until you are ready for the next serving; each person prepares a portion of raclette when so inclined.

If you don't have a fireplace, broil the cheese in the oven. Arrange 1/2-inch-thick slices, side by side, to cover the bottom of a shallow pan. Broil about 4 inches from heat source until melted and bubbling; serve at once. Have pans ready to serve in succession.

Allow at least 2 pounds of cheese for 6 people.

Tiny Boiled Potatoes

Scrub 3 pounds very small new potatoes and boil in water to cover until tender when pierced; takes about 20 minutes. Drain off most of the water and set the potatoes, covered, next to the fire to keep warm during the meal. Makes 6 servings.

Marinated Onions and Pickles

Thinly slice 2 medium-sized mild white onions. Mix with 1/3 cup white wine vinegar, 1/2 teaspoon salt, and 1-1/2 teaspoons sugar. Cover and let chill at least 1 hour; mix occasionally. Also have about 2 cups small sweet pickles. Makes 6 servings.

Mandarin Brunch Party

MANDARIN PANCAKES

ROAST PORK TENDERLOIN

SCRAMBLED EGGS WITH SHRIMP

CHICKEN WITH LEEKS OR GREEN ONION

CONDIMENTS: GREEN ONION SLIVERS,

THIN CARROT STRIPS,

SMALL LEAVES OF

BUTTER LETTUCE,

CHINESE PARSLEY (OR

WATERCRESS),

CRISPY POTATOES, HOT

MUSTARD, HOISIN SAUCE OR

PRESERVED PLUM SAUCE

HOT GREEN TEA

FRESH TANGERINES

This is a sit-down, serve-yourself meal for 4 to 6 guests; each assembles his own mandarin pancakes, selecting filling to enclose in the parchment-thin pancakes. The ingredients for this meal are available in regular grocery stores, but interesting options can be found in Oriental groceries, including Chinese parsley (also called cilantro or coriander), hoisin or plum sauce, and sesame oil (this adds a nut-like flavor to the pancakes).

Some days before the party, you need to devote several hours to making the pancakes. Be sure to follow directions exactly.

Encourage your guests to experiment with the more unusual condiments for fun and interesting results in this new eating experience. Have fillings in the center of the table within easy reach of all.

Mandarin Pancakes

    2   cups unsifted all-purpose flour
    3/4 cup boiling water
    2   tablespoons sesame oil or salad oil

Combine in a bowl the flour, boiling water and 1 tablespoon of the oil; stir with chopsticks or a fork. Work the dough with your hands until it can be formed into a ball. Knead on a lightly floured board until very smooth and velvety, about 10 minutes. Invert a bowl over dough and let it rest for 30 minutes.

Shape the dough into a 12-inch-long log, use a ruler to measure, then cut dough into 12 equal pieces. (From this point on, carefully keep dough and pancakes well covered with clear plastic film to prevent drying.) Have ready a pastry brush and the additional 1 tablespoon oil.

For each pancake, cut a piece of dough in half, form each half piece into a ball, then pat out and roll into a 3-inch circle. Lightly brush top of one circle with oil, fit another circle on top so their edges align, and press together.

Place double piece of dough on a lightly floured board and roll out to a 7 or 8-inch-diameter circle. Keep board lightly floured and turn dough over as needed. Take care to keep from getting creases in the pancakes as you roll. You can form 2 or 3 pancakes this way (keep covered), then cook them before shaping the rest.

To cook the pancakes, heat a wide frying pan over medium-high heat. Place a pancake in the ungreased pan and cook about 15 seconds (it should be blistered all over); then turn and cook about 15 seconds more, or until blistered and slightly translucent. Don't brown. Overcooked, they become dry and brittle. Turn out of pan and immediately separate the 2 layers by gently peeling apart. Stack, and keep covered while making remaining ones. Wrap stack and refrigerate up to 2 days, or freeze.

To reheat pancakes, thaw if frozen, and use a large kettle with rack high enough to keep pancakes well above simmering water or use a steamer. Moisten a tea towel and line steamer or rack. Stack pancakes on towel, then lap edges over pancakes. Cover and steam over simmering water 10 minutes.

Remove part of the pancakes at a time, fold in quarters, and serve in a napkin-lined basket. Leave rest of pancakes in steamer over hot water to keep warm until needed.

Fill with selected tidbits. Makes 4 to 6 servings.

Roast Pork Tenderloin

1   small onion, chopped
1   clove garlic, minced
6   tablespoons soy sauce
2   tablespoons Sherry or Marin (sweet sake)
4   slices fresh ginger root
1   to 1-1/4-pound pork tenderloin (or boned and rolled pork loin)

Combine in a small bowl the onion, garlic, soy sauce, Sherry or Marin, and ginger root. Pour mixture over the pork tenderloin in a deep bowl and refrigerate at least 4 hours or overnight.

Remove meat from marinade and roast, uncovered, in a 375° oven, basting several times with marinade, until a meat thermometer in center registers 175°, about 30 or 40 minutes. Cool, then cut in thin slices and arrange on serving plate. Use as a filling for Mandarin pancakes. Makes 4 to 6 servings.

Scrambled Eggs with Shrimp

8   eggs
1/3 cup milk
3/4 teaspoon salt
1/2 teaspoon grated fresh ginger
6   ounces cooked, shelled tiny shrimp
1/2 cup frozen peas (thawed)
1   tablespoon salad oil

Combine in a bowl the eggs, milk, salt, and fresh ginger. Beat with a fork, cover, and refrigerate until needed. Also have ready the shrimp and peas. Just before serving, heat the salad oil in a frying pan, add egg mixture, and cook over medium heat, stirring gently with a wide spatula, until partly set. Add shrimp and peas and cook about 1 minute, or until softly scrambled. Serve in a warm dish as a Mandarin pancake filling. Makes 4 to 6 servings.

Chicken with Leeks or Green Onion

1   to 1-1/2 pounds chicken breasts or thighs
1   bunch leeks or 2 bunches (12 to 16) green onions
1   teaspoon cornstarch
1/2 teaspoon sugar
1   tablespoon soy sauce
2   tablespoons Sherry or chicken broth
1   tablespoon salad oil

Remove skin and bones from chicken; cut into pieces about 1-1/2 inches square. Wash, trim, and cut coarse tops from leeks or green onions. Cut into 2-1/2-inch lengths, then cut to make strips about 1/4 inch thick.

Arrange chicken and leeks or onions on a plate, cover,

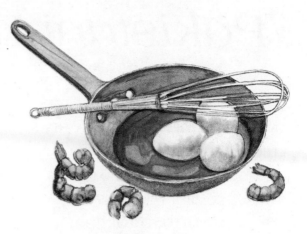

and refrigerate until needed. Also combine in a small pitcher the cornstarch, sugar, soy sauce, and Sherry.

Bring an electric frying pan to the table with the salad oil inside. Heat to 375° and add chicken, then the leeks or onions. Cook, stirring, for 3 or 4 minutes, until chicken turns light color throughout (cut a gash to test) and vegetables are still slightly crisp. Stir soy mixture, add to pan, and cook, stirring, about 1 minute; then reduce heat to warm. Use as a Mandarin pancake filling. Makes 4 to 6 servings.

Condiments

Crisp Vegetables:

Cut 1 large carrot and 2 bunches (12 to 16) green onions (including some of the green tops) into thin slivers, about 2-1/2 inches long. Arrange on serving plate with the pork.

Greens:

Separate tender inner leaves from 2 heads butter lettuce and discard stems from 1 bunch Chinese parsley or watercress. Mound into a bowl or basket.

Crispy Potatoes:

Peel 2 medium-sized potatoes; coarsely shred into a bowl of cold water. Drain, squeeze out water, then dry between towels. In a deep pan, heat 1-1/2 inches of salad oil to 400°. Sprinkle in a handful of potatoes at a time, stirring to prevent clumping; fry until browned, about 2 minutes. Remove with wire strainer; drain on absorbent material. Repeat, bringing oil back to 400° each time. Serve hot; keep cooked potatoes warm until all are ready.

Sauces:

For the hot mustard, blend 1/4 cup dry mustard with enough cold water to make a smooth paste. Hoisin and plum sauces are available in Oriental stores, or substitute chile sauce. Serve in small bowls.

Pakistani Dinner Party

APPETIZERS: BROTH HOT CASHEWS

CHICKEN PULAO CURRIED VEGETABLES

ROAST LEG OF LAMB

CUCUMBER YOGURT SAUCE

HOT BUTTERED TORTILLAS

FRESH FRUIT

POUND CAKE CUSTARD SAUCE (OPTIONAL)

CARDAMOM GREEN TEA

This menu for six, straight from Pakistan, has been slightly adapted to suit the tastes of Westerners; a roast leg of lamb is substituted for the typical whole lamb or goat.

Much preparation can be done in advance. The day before your party, put the lamb to marinate. Butter, wrap, heat tortillas (to approximate Pakistani flat bread) and make the yogurt sauce. Early on the day of the dinner you can start the chicken pulao, prepare vegetables for cooking, and blend broth mixture. Heat the broth just before serving and serve in cups to sip. Accompany with the cashews.

For dessert offer a bowl of whole fruit such as oranges, pineapple, peaches, strawberries, and grapes to be selected and cut for eating as desired. Or instead, serve each person a small plate of the sliced fruit. If you like, accompany fruit with chilled custard sauce made from a mix or your own recipe. For more lavish dessert, offer sliced pound cake with fruit.

Appetizers

Broth:

Blend equal portions regular strength beef broth and tomato juice; season it to taste with Worcestershire and liquid hot pepper seasoning. Allow 1 cup for each serving.

Hot Cashews:

Sprinkle salted cashews with chile powder, drizzle with a little melted butter, and place in a 400° oven just to warm; takes about 2 minutes. Serve hot. Allow about 2 tablespoons for each serving.

Chicken Pulao

    3   tablespoons butter or margarine
    2   medium-sized onions, finely chopped
    2   cloves garlic, crushed
  1/2   chicken breast (6 to 8 oz.) skinned, boned, and diced
    2   cups long grain rice
  1/2   teaspoon salt
    9   whole black peppers
    8   whole cloves
    2   whole cinnamon sticks each 3 to 4 inches long
  1/4   teaspoon ground cardamom
    1   teaspoon grated fresh ginger (or 1/4 teaspoon ground ginger)
3-1/3   cups (about 2 cans 14-oz. size) regular strength chicken broth

Heat butter in a heavy pan over medium heat; add onions, garlic, and chicken breast; sauté 5 minutes. Add rice, salt, peppers, cloves, cinnamon sticks, cardamom, and ginger. (At this point you can cover rice and let stand until about 20 minutes before you want to serve it.)

In a small pan, bring chicken broth to a boil. Pour over rice. Cover and cook over low heat until broth is completely absorbed, about 15 to 20 minutes. Makes about 6 to 8 servings.

Curried Vegetables

These vegetables need careful timing so you won't overcook them. They are flavored with a combination of spices that make the curry rather than a blended curry powder.

    2   tablespoons butter or margarine
    1   medium-sized onion, finely chopped
    2   cloves garlic, crushed
    1   teaspoon salt
  1/2   teaspoon chile powder
    2   teaspoons grated fresh ginger (or 1/2 teaspoon ground ginger)
  1/4   teaspoon each ground cloves and turmeric
    1   small, dried hot chile pepper, crushed
    1   small head cauliflower, broken into small pieces
  1/3   cup regular strength chicken broth
    4   medium-sized zucchini, sliced 1/2 inch thick
    2   medium-sized tomatoes, peeled and diced

Melt butter in a large pan. Add onion, garlic, salt, chile powder, ginger, cloves, turmeric, and hot chile pepper. Sauté until onion is just soft. (At this point, you can cover pan and set aside until about 10 minutes before serving.)

Add cauliflower pieces and chicken broth; cover and

simmer about 4 minutes. Add zucchini; cover and cook 2 to 3 minutes more. Add tomatoes; continue cooking about 1 minute. Remove vegetables to serving dish with slotted spoon; rapidly boil any remaining liquid in the pan until reduced to 3 to 4 tablespoons. Pour liquid over vegetables and serve. Makes 6 servings.

Roast Leg of Lamb

6   to 7-pound bone-in leg of lamb
1   cup soy sauce
1   tablespoon grated fresh ginger
1/2 cup salad oil
4   cloves garlic, crushed

For carving ease, have lamb boned, rolled, and tied, if you wish. For the marinade, combine soy sauce, ginger, salad oil, and garlic. Put the lamb in a large shallow pan. Pour marinade over meat, cover, and refrigerate about 24 hours, turning meat occasionally. To roast, lift meat from marinade and place on a rack in a shallow roasting pan; roast, uncovered, in a 325° oven 2 to 2-1/2 hours for a bone-in leg, about 2-1/2 to 2-3/4 hours for a boneless rolled leg. A meat thermometer inserted in center of thickest muscle will register 160° for medium rare. Makes 6 servings.

Cucumber Yogurt Sauce

Serve this sauce to spoon onto portions of lamb, curried vegetables, and the chicken pulao.

2   cups unflavored yogurt (maybe part sour cream)
1   small cucumber, peeled and shredded
1/2 cup chopped green onion
1/2 teaspoon each salt and sugar
1   teaspoon ground cumin
1/4 teaspoon chile powder
1   package (10 oz.) frozen peas

Combine yogurt with cucumber, onion, salt, sugar, cumin, and chile powder. Cook frozen peas as directed on the package; drain thoroughly. Add peas to the yogurt mixture and refrigerate sauce for several hours or overnight to blend flavors. Makes 3 cups.

Cardamom-Flavored Green Tea

Add 6 whole cardamom seeds, crushed, and 1 (3 or 4 inches long) cinnamon stick, broken, to 6 servings of tea when you steep it.

Japanese One-Dish

DASHI

ONIGARI YAKI

RICE   EDIBLE PEA PODS

TEA

Seat guests comfortably on mats around low-to-the-floor tables to eat this meal. For Dashi, buy packages labeled "Dashi-no-Moto soup stock" either in tea-like bags or cubes. Follow package directions.

Onigari Yaki

This dish could be classified as a *teriyaki* "glaze-broiled" dish and is cooked over charcoal.

1/2 cup Sherry or sweet rice wine
1   cup soy sauce
1   tablespoon sugar
36 large raw shrimp (about 3 lbs.), peeled and deveined
    Hot cooked long-grained rice

In a small saucepan, combine wine, soy sauce, and sugar; bring to a boil.
Thread 6 shrimp on individual skewers. Dip skewers in combined sauce and broil over hot coals (or under a broiler). Brush constantly with sauce until glazed and bright pink, a few minutes on each side. Serve over hot cooked rice. Makes 4 servings.

The Party for

a Few Guests

One of the most gracious ways to entertain is a dinner for a small group. The well-organized hostess can anticipate joining in the lively conversation that such intimate gatherings invite. You will find ample guidance in this chapter for planning and preparing the foods. You can choose to serve formally, in courses, with the quiet elegance suggested in the menu featuring the au gratin of sole; with the jovial spirit of participation required by the dramatically presented cracked crab party; or informally, perhaps even as a moonlight picnic, the corned beef dinner on trays. There are a multitude of ideas for all ranges of party styles with many suggestions for steps to complete in advance, as well as how to serve the meal.

A candlelit dinner for two or three couples features a roast goose handsomely presented on a large silver tray with vegetables and fruit. The salad and cheese follow. Menu and recipes can be found on pages 14-15.

A Springtime Dinner Party

SPRING POTATO SOUP

STUFFED CABBAGE ROLLS

GRILLED LAMB RIBLETS

MINTED CITRUS SALAD

DARK RYE BREAD

IMPERIAL MOUSSE

Springtime brings fair weather and once again you can make use of your garden for an entertaining center. Combine soup ingredients ahead of time; heat to serve. Start cooking the lamb an hour before serving dinner. Stuff cabbage ahead ready to simmer while lamb cooks. Make salad dressing and prepare salad fruits and greens; arrange and dress salad at the last minute. The dessert can be made the night before and chilled.

Spring Potato Soup

1   can (10-1/4 oz.) condensed potato soup
1   can (about 14 oz.) regular strength chicken broth
1-1/2   cups milk
    Green onion tops, thinly sliced

Combine potato soup, chicken broth, and milk. Whirl smooth in a blender. Heat (or just combine ingredients and heat); sprinkle each serving with thin rings of green onion tops. Makes 6 servings.

Stuffed Cabbage Rolls

12   medium-sized cabbage leaves
     Boiling water
3   cups finely chopped cabbage
1/4 cup minced onion
4   tablespoons (1/4 cup) butter or margarine
1-1/2   cups cooked rice
6   tablespoons grated Romano or Parmesan cheese
     Salt
1/2 teaspoon freshly ground pepper
1-1/4   cups tomato juice

Immerse cabbage leaves in boiling water to cover for about 3 minutes. Lift out and drain. Sauté chopped cabbage and minced onion in butter until limp and tender. Add rice, cheese, salt to taste, and pepper. Divide this mixture evenly among the cabbage leaves. Fold in sides and roll to enclose filling; fasten with toothpicks. To

heat and serve, place rolls in a single layer in a shallow saucepan, add tomato juice, and simmer for 20 minutes. Makes 6 servings.

Grilled Lamb Riblets

5   pounds lamb riblets (about 3/4 pound or 4 to 5 ribs per serving)
3/4 teaspoon each seasoned salt, garlic salt, salt, and pepper
2   tablespoons Worcestershire

Cut lamb riblets between each rib. Arrange in a single layer on a broiler rack. Combine remaining ingredients; brush on lamb. Place lamb about 6 inches below heat source and broil 20 to 30 minutes, turning to brown, on all sides. Place in a 375° oven and bake for 30 minutes. Serve hot to eat as finger food. Makes 6 servings.

Minted Citrus Salad

2   cups fresh grapefruit sections
2   or 3 large oranges, peeled and thinly sliced
     Salad greens, butter lettuce leaves or romaine leaves
     Mint leaves
3   tablespoons mint jelly
1   tablespoon honey
     Grated peel and juice of 1 lime
     Juice of 1 lemon

Arrange grapefruit sections and orange slices on a bed of salad greens on individual serving plates or in a large salad bowl. Garnish with mint leaves. Blend together mint jelly, honey, grated lime peel, lime juice, and lemon juice. Ladle some of the dressing on each serving. Makes 6 servings.

Imperial Mousse

1   envelope unflavored gelatin
1/2 cup cold water
1/2 cup boiling water
2   cups (1 pt.) sour cream
1/2 cup sugar
1/2 teaspoon almond extract
1   teaspoon vanilla
     Pineapple ice cream sauce, fresh crushed berries, or jelly or jam

Soften gelatin in cold water. Add boiling water and stir until gelatin is dissolved. Blend in sour cream, sugar, almond extract, and vanilla. Pour into a 1-quart mold. Chill until firm, about 3 hours. Dip mold in hot tap water up to rim until mousse begins to melt around edges. Unmold and serve with pineapple ice cream sauce, fresh crushed berries, or jelly or jam of your choice. Makes 6 servings.

A Small Dinner Party

ANCHOVY TURNOVERS

FRESH VEGETABLE STICKS

VEAL SCALOPPINE

SLICED ZUCCHINI ROUNDS

TWO-TONE RICE

PEARS WITH ZABAGLIONE

Savory fresh baked pastries are an effortless opening for this party; you chill the shaped turnovers and bake at the last minute.

Anchovy Turnovers

1   small package (3 oz.) cream cheese, cut in chunks
1/2   cup (1/4 lb.) butter or margarine, cut in chunks
1   cup all-purpose flour, unsifted
    About 3/4 tube (2 oz. size) anchovy paste

With your fingers work cheese and butter into flour until evenly blended. With your hand compress dough into a ball. Chill for about 2 hours. On a floured board roll dough 1/8 inch thick and cut into 2-inch rounds. Put about 1/4 teaspoon anchovy paste in the center of each round. Moisten edges and press together, turn-over fashion. Prick tops. Reroll dough as needed until all is shaped. Place on baking sheet and chill, covered, until serving time. Bake in a 375° oven 10 minutes or until golden brown. Serve at once. Makes about 3 dozen.

Veal Scaloppine

2   to 2-1/2 pounds boneless veal cutlets, thinly sliced
    All-purpose flour
    Salt and pepper
3   tablespoons each olive oil and butter
1   lemon, very thinly sliced
3   tablespoons lemon juice
1   clove garlic, minced
2   tablespoons minced parsley
1/4   cup water
    Salt to taste

Trim any membrane from veal. Place meat between sheets of waxed paper and pound until about 1/4 inch thick. Coat meat with flour and shake off excess;

sprinkle lightly with salt and pepper. Heat about half the oil and butter in a wide frying pan over medium-high heat. Brown the meat on all sides; do not crowd pan and add more oil and butter as needed. Remove cooked meat to a platter and keep warm. In a pan, turn lemon slices in drippings, then add lemon juice to pan along with garlic juice, parsley, and water. On high heat bring to a boil, stirring the crusty bits from the pan. Pour over the meat. Makes 6 servings.

Two-Toned Rice

3/4   cup each long grain rice and well washed wild rice
3   cups condensed consommé
2   tablespoons each soy sauce and minced onion

Place white rice in a 1-quart baking dish in a 350° oven to toast 20 minutes until golden brown. Meanwhile, bring 1-1/2 cups of the consommé to boiling, add wild rice and simmer, covered 10 minutes. Stir remaining 1-1/2 cups consommé, soy sauce, minced onion, and partially cooked wild rice in with white rice. Cover and bake in a 350° oven 35 to 40 minutes. Makes 6 servings.

Pears with Zabaglione

6   ripe pears
2   cups sugar
1   cup water
1   teaspoon vanilla
4   egg yolks
3   tablespoons sugar
4   tablespoons Marsala or dry Sherry
    Toasted slivered almonds

Peel pears, cut in half, and core. Boil 2 cups sugar, the water, and vanilla, stirring, until clear. Add pears and simmer 5 minutes. Chill in syrup. At serving time lift pears from syrup and place 2 halves in each individual dish.

For the sauce, put egg yolks in the top of a double boiler and add the 3 tablespoons sugar and the Marsala. Place mixture over simmering water, beating constantly with a rotary mixer or wire whip until thick and foamy, about 5 minutes. Remove from heat at once and pour evenly over pears. Sprinkle with toasted slivered almonds. Serve at once. Makes 6 servings.

Patio Dinner Party

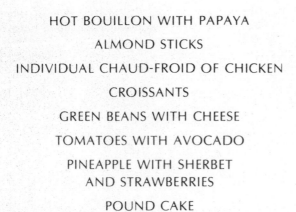

HOT BOUILLON WITH PAPAYA

ALMOND STICKS

INDIVIDUAL CHAUD-FROID OF CHICKEN

CROISSANTS

GREEN BEANS WITH CHEESE

TOMATOES WITH AVOCADO

PINEAPPLE WITH SHERBET
AND STRAWBERRIES

POUND CAKE

The chicken is served chilled, so it can be made well ahead of time. You can make the almond sticks several hours ahead and chill. Make and chill avocado topping for tomatoes; assemble just before serving. Also fill pineapple shells with sherbet and freeze firm. Bake the pound cake a day ahead or buy a frozen one.

Hot Bouillon with Papaya

    3   cans (10-1/2 oz. each) condensed beef bouillon
    3/4 cup water
    2   tablespoons lime or lemon juice
    1/2 ripe papaya, peeled and cut into small cubes

Combine bouillon, water, and lime or lemon juice. Heat to boiling and pour into cups. Garnish each serving with small cubes of papaya. Makes 6 servings.

Almond Sticks

    3   slices fresh white bread
    1   small package (3 oz.) cream cheese
    1   tablespoon milk
    1/2 teaspoon curry powder
    1/2 teaspoon lemon juice
    1/2 can (about 7-1/2 oz. size) salted almonds, chopped

Remove crusts from bread. Cut each slice in thirds, then cut each section in half. Cream the cheese with milk, curry powder, and lemon juice. Spread cheese mixture on all sides of bread sticks. Roll in chopped salted almonds and chill until time to serve with the hot bouillon. Makes 18 almond sticks.

Individual Chaud-Froid of Chicken

Chaud-froid gets its name from a combination of warm sauce and a cold glaze used to coat cold fowl or meat.

    4   tablespoons each all-purpose flour and melted butter
    2-1/2 cups regular strength chicken broth
    1   cup whipping cream
    1   tablespoon lemon juice
        Salt and white pepper
    3   envelopes unflavored gelatin
    1/4 cup cold water
    6   whole large (about 1 lb. each) chicken breasts, split, cooked, skinned, and boned
    12 to 16 cold cooked or canned boiling onions
        Sliced ripe olives
        Chive spears, minced parsley or paprika

Blend together flour and melted butter. Stir in 1-1/2 cups of the chicken broth, whipping cream, and lemon juice. Season to taste with salt and white pepper. Bring to a boil and cook, stirring, until smooth and thick. Soften 2 envelopes of the gelatin in 1/4 cup of the cold water; then dissolve in the hot sauce. Cool, stirring occasionally until consistency of softly whipped cream, but do not allow to set.

Arrange chicken breasts and onions on 6 plates or a serving platter. Evenly spoon chaud-froid sauce over the chicken and onions. Decorate breasts at once with slices of olives and chive spears; sprinkle onions with minced parsley or paprika. Chill.

Soften the remaining gelatin in the remaining 1 cup broth; heat, stirring, until gelatin is dissolved. Then chill until slightly syrupy; pour carefully over the decorated breasts to glaze. Chill until ready to serve. Makes 6 servings.

Green Beans with Cheese

    1-1/2 pounds green beans, ends and strings removed
        Boiling water
    1   clove garlic
    1   teaspoon salt
    1/4 cup melted butter
    1/4 teaspoon crushed basil
    3   tablespoons grated Parmesan cheese
    2   tablespoons fine dry bread crumbs blended with 1 tablespoon melted butter

Cook beans, uncovered, in boiling water to cover with garlic and salt on high heat for about 7 minutes after boil resumes or until tender but still crisp and green;

drain well; discard garlic. Mix beans with the 1/4 cup melted butter, basil, and cheese. Sprinkle with buttered crumbs. Serve at once. Makes 6 servings.

Tomatoes with Avocado

1   large or 2 small avocados
2   tablespoons minced canned California green chiles
2   tablespoons mayonnaise
1   teaspoon lemon juice
2   teaspoons grated onion
    Salt
    About 1/3 cup minced celery
3   medium-sized tomatoes
    Lettuce
    Additional mayonnaise or sour cream

Mash avocados, and mix with chiles, the 2 tablespoons mayonnaise, lemon juice, grated onion, salt, and celery. Cover and chill if made ahead. Cut tomatoes in halves;

set each half on a lettuce leaf, top with equal portions of the avocado sauce, then with a small spoonful of mayonnaise. Makes 6 servings.

Pineapple with Sherbet and Strawberries

1   large ripe pineapple
1   quart lemon, pineapple, raspberry, or boysenberry sherbet
1   quart strawberries (or other seasonal berries)
    Sugar
    Mint sprigs, flowers

Cut pineapple in half lengthwise, through the crown. Scoop out the fruit with a grapefruit knife; dice fruit and set aside. Discard core. Mound sherbet into shells and freeze. To serve mix pineapple with strawberries and sweeten to taste with sugar. Present shells with sherbet on a tray garnished with mint and blossoms. Scoop sherbet into dessert bowls and pass fruit to spoon on top. Makes 6 to 8 servings.

Cracked Crab Party

WINTER TOMATO SOUP

CRACKED CRAB PLATTER

AVOCADO CREAM DIP

PIQUANT MAYONNAISE DRESSING

HOT DEVILED BUTTER

RELISH KEBABS

TOASTED FRENCH BREAD FINGERS

APPLE TARTS WITH HOT LEMON SAUCE

The light vegetable soup, steaming hot, is a perfect prelude to the chilled crab. The delicate flavor of cracked fresh crab can best be appreciated "as is", or with just the right sauce or dip to enhance its flavor. This menu offers a choice of one hot sauce and two cold ones. Assorted relishes and crusty hot French bread are the only other accompaniments.

Provide each guest with a pick or show them how to use the slender tip of a crab leg to pluck the white meat from the shells. Have a basket or wooden bowl

to hold discarded shells. Provide finger bowls or hot wet towels for freshening up as needed.

Winter Tomato Soup

1/2   cup chopped celery
2   tablespoons butter or fresh bacon drippings
1   can (1 lb.) stewed tomatoes
1   can (10-1/2 oz.) condensed consommé or condensed chicken broth
1/2   cup dry white wine or 1/2 cup additional chicken broth
3   tablespoons chopped green onion or 1 tablespoon instant minced onion
1   tablespoon lemon juice
1   tablespoon cornstarch, blended with 1/2 cup water
      Dash curry powder (to taste)
      Cheese croutons (optional)

Sauté the celery in butter or bacon drippings until soft, about 5 minutes over medium heat. Add tomatoes, consommé, wine, onion, lemon juice, and cornstarch mixture; blend well. Add curry powder to taste. Simmer 15 to 20 minutes, stirring occasionally. Garnish with cheese croutons, if you wish. Makes 6 servings.

Cracked Crab Platter

You can estimate that a 1-1/4 to 1-1/2-pound crab will serve 1 person very well or that a 2-1/2 to 3-1/2-pound crab will serve two people quite generously. You can have the fresh cooked crabs cleaned and cracked at the market where you buy them, or do this yourself. Reserve one large crab whole.

It is very attractive to arrange cracked crab on a mound of cracked ice. Choose a large platter or tray that is deep enough to collect the water as the ice melts. Divide the crabs into parts: main body sections, large legs, and smaller legs. Keep the various parts separate, alternating them on the platter. Finally, center the reserved whole crab on top of the mound.

For added embellishment, spear a collection of relishes (lemon wedges, fancy pickles, cherry tomatoes, and green stuffed olives) on skewers, and stick them into the crab shell at the very top of the pile. Garnish the platter with parsley or crisp romaine leaves.

Avocado-Cream Dip

    2 medium-sized avocados
  1/2 cup sour cream
    2 tablespoons each lime or lemon juice, or dry
       white wine, and chopped green onion
    1 teaspoon seasoned salt
  1/8 teaspoon garlic powder
    1 chopped small canned hot green jalapeño chile
       (optional)
    1 medium-sized tomato, peeled and chopped

Peel and remove pits from avocados. Place avocado in a blender with sour cream, lime or lemon juice or white wine, green onion, seasoned salt, garlic powder, and green chile. Cover and whirl until fairly smooth (or mash avocado with a fork and blend in remaining ingredients). Stir in tomato. Cover and chill until ready to serve. Makes 2 cups or 6 to 8 servings.

Piquant Mayonnaise Dressing

  3/4 cup mayonnaise
    1 cup (1/2 pt.) sour cream
    2 tablespoons each chile (tomato based) sauce, chopped
       dill pickle, chopped green pepper, and chopped
       green onion
    1 tablespoon each chopped canned pimiento and
       wine vinegar
  1/4 cup dry white wine or light cream
    2 hard-cooked eggs, chopped
       Salt

Blend mayonnaise with sour cream, chile sauce, dill pickle, green pepper, green onion, pimiento, vinegar, wine, eggs, and salt to taste. Mix, cover, and chill for several hours before serving. Makes 2 cups or 6 to 8 servings.

Hot Deviled Butter

    1 cup (1/2 lb.) butter
    2 teaspoons each Worcestershire and prepared mustard
    2 tablespoons chile (tomato based) sauce
    2 to 3 drops liquid hot pepper seasoning
    4 teaspoons lemon or lime juice
    2 to 3 teaspoons finely chopped parsley

Combine in a small pan or chafing dish the butter, Worcestershire, mustard, chile sauce, liquid hot pepper seasoning, lemon juice, and parsley. When ready to serve heat until bubbly; to serve at table keep chafing dish over a low flame and pour into small bowls at table as desired. Makes about 1 cup or 6 to 8 servings.

Toasted French Bread Fingers

Some like the flavor of garlic-buttered French bread with crab, others prefer the crusty bread simply buttered and toasted. Cut a long loaf (l lb. size) in half lengthwise and butter each half generously; sprinkle lightly with garlic powder, if desired. Toast the bread halves under the broiler, then use scissors to cut each crosswise into fingers. Serve hot.

Apple Tarts with Hot Lemon Sauce

For the dessert, make tarts, using your favorite recipe for apple pie; or you may prefer to buy the tarts at your bakery. Serve with Lemon Sauce.

Lemon Sauce:

  1/3 cup sugar
    1 tablespoon cornstarch
    1 cup boiling water
    2 teaspoons grated lemon peel
    2 tablespoons each lemon juice and butter

Combine sugar and cornstarch in a saucepan; stir in water and lemon peel. Stirring, bring to a boil and cook until slightly thickened and clear. Remove from heat; stir in lemon juice and butter. Serve warm or reheated. Makes about 1 cup, or topping for 6 to 8 desserts.

Crown Roast Spectacular

The crown roast of lamb pictured on the cover of this book can also be served with fresh mint and herb stuffing to make a most imposing entrée.

Crown Roast of Lamb with Mint Stuffing

5	to 6-pound crown roast of lamb
1/4	cup thinly sliced celery
2	tablespoons chopped onion
6	tablespoons butter
3	cups soft bread crumbs
1	egg
2	tablespoons water
1/3	cup finely chopped fresh mint leaves
1/2	teaspoon each finely chopped fresh sage, marjoram, and thyme (or 1/4 teaspoon each of these dried herbs)
	Salt and pepper
	Paper chop frills (ask your meatman for them)
	Spiced whole red crab apples

Place roast on rack in a pan. Prepare stuffing: Sauté celery and onion in butter until soft. Remove from heat; add crumbs, the egg beaten with the water, mint, sage, marjoram, thyme, and mix with a fork. Salt and pepper to taste. Lightly pack into the well in the center of the roast. Bake in a 325° oven for about 3-1/2 hours, or about 40 minutes per pound. Top the ends of rib bones with paper chop frills. Garnish with crab apples. Cut between ribs to serve. Makes about 6 servings.

Asparagus with Brown Butter

Cook 3 pounds asparagus, trimmed of tough ends, according to directions on page 53. Drain, season with salt and pepper, and arrange in serving dish. Pour over 1/3 cup butter which has been heated until brown and bubbling.

Boysenberry Puff Torte

1-1/3	cups unsifted all-purpose flour
10	tablespoons butter
2	tablespoons sugar
2/3	cup water
3	eggs
1	cup whipping cream
4	cups boysenberries, sugared to taste (or other fresh berries such as strawberries or raspberries)

In a bowl combine 2/3 cup of the flour, 5 tablespoons of the butter, and the 2 tablespoons sugar. Rub mixture with your fingers until it is mealy. Pour into a 9-inch cake pan with removable bottom; press firmly in an even layer.

In a saucepan, combine water and remaining 5 tablespoons butter. Quickly bring to a boil, stirring to melt butter. Dump in remaining 2/3 cup flour all at once, take pan from heat, and stir until mixture is smooth. Beat in eggs, one at a time, until mixture is smooth and glossy. Gently spread over the butter-flour layer in cake pan.

Bake in a 400° oven for 1 hour 5 minutes, or until topping is irregularly puffed and well browned; turn off heat and leave in closed oven 10 minutes longer to dry. Remove pan rim and let torte cool; the puff will settle slightly.

To serve, whip cream until stiff and spread on top of puff, then pile berries into the cream; cut in wedges. Makes 8 to 10 servings.

Entertaining
with Roast Chicken

This elegant roast chicken dinner is to be served as a four-course affair: the appetizer; the chilled crab cocktail; the entrée with vegetables; and the dessert with coffee.

Artichoke Appetizer

2   small packages (3 oz. each) cream cheese
1   small clove garlic, minced
1/4   cup sour cream
2   teaspoons wine vinegar
1/4   cup minced ripe olives
    Salt
3   large cold cooked artichokes, bracts separated
    from bases

Mash cream cheese and garlic smoothly with sour cream. Blend in vinegar, olives, and salt to taste, chill. On each of 6 individual salad plates arrange an equal number of artichoke bracts (or leaves) point towards plate rim in several overlapping layers to make a wreath; put 1/2 an artichoke bottom on each plate. Place a small bowl with some of the sauce in the center. Cover and chill if made ahead. Makes 6 servings.

Crab and Avocado Cocktail

2   large ripe avocados
1/2   pound flaked crab and 6 crab legs
1/2   cup mayonnaise
2   teaspoons lemon juice
1   tablespoon half-and-half
    Additional mayonnaise

Peel, pit, and dice avocados. Mix crab (reserve legs) with the 1/2 cup mayonnaise, lemon juice, and cream. Mix lightly with diced avocado and put in cocktail glasses. (Cover and chill for 1 to 2 hours if made ahead.) Top each serving with a small spoonful of mayonnaise and a crab leg. Makes 6 servings.

Roast Chicken

Select a 5-pound roasting chicken. Bake, breast side up, on a rack in a roasting pan in a 325° oven for 2-1/2 hours, or until drumstick moves easily. Baste occasionally with melted butter (about 3 tablespoons total). Makes 6 servings.

Gingered Carrots

2   pounds carrots, peeled
    Salted water
4   tablespoons (1/4 cup) butter
1   tablespoon minced candied ginger or grated
    fresh ginger

Cook carrots until tender in boiling salted water to cover; drain. (This can be done ahead.) Put carrots in a wide frying pan with butter and ginger, and cook, stirring, until lightly browned. Makes 6 servings.

New Potatoes

Boil 3 pounds potatoes in their skins in water to cover until tender to pierce; drain. Roll in 1/4 cup melted butter, then in 1/2 cup minced watercress. Makes 6 servings.

Strawberry Ring Shortcake

Prepare 2 cups baking mix according to package directions for rolled biscuits, adding 3 tablespoons sugar and 2 tablespoons melted butter. Arrange biscuits, overlapping, in a buttered 8- or 9-inch ring mold. Bake in a 475° oven for 8 to 10 minutes. Invert onto a serving plate. Sweeten 1 quart fresh, hulled, sliced strawberries with 1/2 cup sugar and pour into center of biscuit ring. Serve hot with sauce of 1-1/2 cups sour cream blended with 1/3 cup honey. Makes 6 to 8 servings.

Serving Tray Entertaining

CHICKEN AND CUCUMBER SOUP

SLICED CORNED BEEF

FRENCH POTATO SALAD

ASPARAGUS VINAIGRETTE

RIPE OLIVES   CARROT STICKS

SOUR FRENCH ROLLS

FRUIT TURNOVERS

If you are having a few friends in to watch the big game or for an uninterrupted evening of bridge, you can present this dinner when you please. Bring in the first course with soup in bowls or to ladle from a small tureen into sipping mugs. Carry away the remains of this hand-held course and present the corned beef tray with all the extras. Buy, or bake ahead, fruit turnovers and pass them when everyone is ready for coffee.

A good chunk of corned beef, which needs to simmer slowly for about 4 hours, is the keystone of this service. After cooking liquid develops meaty flavors, you tuck in the potatoes for salad to cook alongside the meat. Then use the cooking liquid to cook asparagus. All the cooking for this dinner can be done a day ahead, or be started first thing in the morning.

Chicken and Cucumber Soup

1   can (10-1/2 oz.) condensed cream of chicken soup
1   soup can water
1   can (about 14 oz.) regular strength chicken broth
1   medium-sized cucumber
1/4   cup finely chopped onion
    Salt and pepper

Empty soup into a saucepan. Gradually stir in water, then stir in chicken broth. Cut 6 very thin slices from an unpeeled cucumber and set aside for garnish; then peel and finely chop remaining cucumber.

Add chopped cucumber to the soup along with onion; cover and chill if you make it ahead.

To serve, heat to boiling point, then simmer for 1 minute. Add salt and pepper to taste. Garnish each bowl with one of the reserved cucumber slices. Makes about 6 servings.

Sliced Corned Beef

In a 6-quart or larger kettle, place a 3-1/2 to 4-1/2-pound piece of corned beef round and water to just cover meat. Add 1 bay leaf, 1 thick slice onion, and 4 whole black peppers, and simmer until beef is fork tender, about 4 hours, turning over once.

Remove beef from cooking liquid, and cool until you can handle it. Trim off any excess fat from meat, wrap, and refrigerate until cold. Cut in thin slices to arrange on serving tray along with French potato salad and asparagus vinaigrette (directions follow). Makes 6 to 8 servings.

French Potato Salad

Scrub well 2 pounds medium-sized new white potatoes. Cook them in with the corned beef or in boiling salted water until just tender when pierced with a fork, about 25 minutes. Remove from broth with a slotted spoon.

As soon as potatoes cool enough to handle but while still warm, peel them, cut in halves lengthwise, then slice thinly crosswise and put into a bowl. Add 1/3 cup thinly sliced green onions, including some tops, and 1/4 cup bottled Italian dressing. Mix gently, cover, and refrigerate for at least 1 hour.

Before serving, again mix gently and add salt and pepper to taste, and additional dressing if needed. Garnish the bowl with lettuce when you serve. Makes about 6 servings.

Asparagus Vinaigrette

Wash and snap off tough ends from 2 pounds asparagus; cook in a wide, uncovered, frying pan until just tender in about 1 inch of corned beef cooking liquid or in boiling salted water. Drain, then chill. About 30 minutes before serving time, sprinkle with about 1/4 cup bottled Italian dressing. Arrange on the tray just before serving. Makes about 6 servings.

An Elegant Dinner

PAPAYA OR CANTALOUPE WITH DRY SALAMI

FILLET OF SOLE FLORENTINE AU GRATIN

BARLEY AND PINE NUT PILAF

A FAVORITE GREEN SALAD CLASSIC

MACADAMIA TORTONI

When guests arrive, dinner preparations are out of the way. All that remains to be done is to take foods out of the refrigerator, freezer, and oven. You might prepare a salad, such as a Caesar salad, at the table as a separate course; or simply mix a dressing such as Green Goddess or a piquant oil and vinegar and blend with selected salad greens.

Papaya or Cantaloupe with Dry Salami

Peel and seed large papaya or small cantaloupe and cut in slender wedges, arranging with thinly sliced salami (allow 2 or 3 pieces for a serving) on a platter or as individual servings. Eat with forks. Makes 4 to 6 servings.

Fillet of Sole Florentine au Gratin

2	packages (10 oz. each) frozen chopped spinach
6	large (at least 2 lbs.) sole fillets
1/2	cup Madeira or dry Sherry
2	tablespoons lemon juice
	Salt
	Water
2	tablespoons each butter and all-purpose flour
1/2	teaspoon chicken stock base
1/2	teaspoon Dijon-style mustard
1/3	cup whipping cream
3/4	cup shredded Swiss cheese

Set out frozen chopped spinach to thaw. Fold sole fillets in half and arrange side by side in a shallow baking pan. Mix Madeira or Sherry and lemon juice and pour over the fish. Sprinkle lightly with salt and bake in a 350° oven for 15 minutes. Remove from oven, drain off all the liquid and measure; cover fish and chill. Add enough water to the fish broth to make 1 cup.

Melt butter in a saucepan and stir in flour, chicken stock, and the mustard. Gradually add the fish broth mixture and whipping cream. Cook, stirring until bubbling and thickened. Stir in 1/2 cup of the shredded Swiss cheese. Cover sauce and chill as long as overnight.

Squeeze all liquid possible from spinach and distribute the spinach evenly in a shallow 1-1/2-quart casserole; arrange the cooked and chilled sole fillets on top. Cover and chill.

Just before serving time, reheat sauce until bubbling and spoon evenly over fish. Sprinkle with the remaining Swiss cheese. Bake in a 450° oven for 15 to 18 minutes or until bubbling slightly, then broil briefly to brown top lightly. Makes 6 servings.

Barley and Pine Nut Pilaf

1	cup pearl barley
6	tablespoons butter or margarine
1/4	to 1/2 cup pine nuts or slivered almonds
1	medium-sized onion, chopped
1/2	cup minced parsley
1/4	cup minced chives or green onions
1/4	teaspoon each salt and pepper
2	cans (about 14 oz. each) regular strength beef broth or chicken broth
	Parsley for garnish

Rinse the barley in cold water and drain well. In a wide frying pan, melt 2 tablespoons of the butter over medium heat. Add pine nuts and stir until lightly toasted. Remove the nuts with a slotted spoon and set aside. Add remaining 4 tablespoons butter to pan along with onion and drained barley; cook, stirring, until lightly toasted. Remove from heat, stir in the pine nuts, parsley, chives, salt, and pepper. Spoon into a 1-1/2-quart casserole. (This much may be done ahead; cover and chill.)

Heat the broth to boiling, pour over barley mixture in casserole, and stir to blend well. Bake, uncovered, in a 375° oven until the barley is tender and most liquid is absorbed, about 1 hour and 10 minutes. (If you have only one oven keep warm while the sole finishes cooking.) Garnish with parsley. Makes 4 to 6 servings.

Macadamia Tortoni

   1   *cup salted macadamias*
   5   *tablespoons butter*
1/2   *cup plus 2 tablespoons sugar*
1/4   *cup water*
   2   *eggs yolks*
3/4   *cup whipping cream*

Roll macadamias in a cloth to remove some of the salt. Then lift nuts from the cloth. Melt 1 tablespoon of the butter in a frying pan. Add nuts, and 2 tablespoons of the sugar. Cook over moderate heat, stirring, until nuts begin to brown slightly. Set aside to cool.

Boil together the 1/2 cup sugar and water, stirring occasionally, until mixture is clear. At the same time beat egg yolks until they begin to thicken; then beat in the hot syrup, adding in a slow steady stream avoiding the beaters. Cut the remaining 4 tablespoons butter in small pieces and beat into egg mixture a few lumps at a time. Chill.

Chop nuts into pieces about as big as 1/6 of a large nut. Whip cream until stiff and fold nuts and cream into the cold egg mixture. Pour into 6 to 8 paper-lined muffin cups (or 6 individual dishes). Freeze; cover airtight when solid. Let mellow about 5 minutes at room temperature before serving. Makes 6 to 8 servings.

A Last Minute Party

FRENCH ONION SOUP

TOASTED CRAB MUFFINS

GARBANZO AND BEET SALAD

LEMON SHERBET

You can make the soup ahead and reheat it, or use canned or packaged soup; while it heats, assemble sandwiches and broil; you can easily double recipe if you want more than one open-face sandwich for each person. For the salad have canned garbanzos and sliced beets well chilled. Drain garbanzos and sliced beets and arrange with halved cherry tomatoes on a serving dish lined with lettuce leaves; spoon over bottled Italian dressing.

French Onion Soup

The secret of this soup is to sauté onions very slowly until they take on a rich caramel color.

   3   *large onions, thinly sliced*
1/4   *cup butter*
   2   *teaspoons all-purpose flour*
   6   *cups regular strength beef broth (canned or homemade)*
1/3   *cup dry white wine*
      Salt and pepper

Sauté onion over medium-low heat in butter in a kettle for about 30 to 40 minutes, stirring frequently. Sprinkle onions with flour and stir to blend. Slowly stir in beef broth and bring to a boil and simmer, uncovered, for 15 minutes. Add white wine. Taste broth and season, if needed, with salt and pepper. Serve hot or chill, then reheat. Makes 6 to 8 servings.

Toasted Crab Muffins

   1   *small package (3 oz.) cream cheese*
   1   *tablespoon milk*
   2   *teaspoons lemon juice*
      Several dashes liquid hot pepper seasoning
   2   *green onions, finely chopped*
   8   *ounces fresh or 1 can (7-1/2 oz.) crab meat*
   3   *or 4 English muffins, split*
      Butter

Beat the cream cheese together with the milk, lemon juice, and several dashes liquid hot pepper seasoning. Mix in the onions and crab meat. Split, butter, and toast the English muffins and spread cheese filling over the hot toasted sides. Broil just until top browns slightly. Makes 6 to 8 open-faced sandwiches.

Grilled Salmon Dinner

ICED CUCUMBER SOUP

GRILLED SALMON STEAKS

BROCCOLI WITH HOLLANDAISE

HOT ROLLS

LEMON CREAM CHEESE TARTS

The chilled cucumber soup is a perfect prelude to the grilled salmon. Accompaniments are simple: Fresh broccoli with hollandaise sauce; homemade yeast rolls (perhaps from a mix) or frozen heated brioche; and light lemon cream cheese tarts to top off the dinner.

Iced Cucumber Soup

3   large cucumbers
1   small white onion
3   tablespoons butter or margarine
3   tablespoons all-purpose flour
2-1/2 cups regular strength chicken broth (chicken stock base or chicken bouillon cubes may be used)
1   teaspoon dill weed
2   teaspoons lemon juice
2   cups half-and-half
     Salt and pepper to taste
1   teaspoon dill weed

Peel and split cucumbers, remove and discard seeds, and chop. Chop onion, combine with cucumber, and sauté in butter in a wide frying pan until soft. Stir in flour, then chicken broth, the 1 teaspoon dill weed, and the lemon juice.

Cook until thickened, then whirl in blender or press through a fine wire strainer. Combine with half-and-half, and season to taste with salt and pepper. Chill. Serve very cold, topped with a light sprinkling of more dill weed. Makes 6 to 8 servings.

Broccoli with Hollandaise

Trim tough ends from 3 pounds broccoli. Drop broccoli into a large pan of boiling salted water and cook uncovered 3 to 4 minutes after boil resumes on high heat or until stem ends of broccoli are just tender to pierce. Drain and serve with hollandaise (see page 53 for recipe or warm 1 to 1-1/4 cups canned hollandaise). Makes 6 to 8 servings.

Grilled Salmon Steaks

Arrange 6 to 8 salmon steaks (each about 3/4 inch thick) on a broiler rack. Broil 4-1/2 to 5 inches from heat, basting occasionally with 3 to 4 tablespoons melted butter, for about 8 minutes or until fish flakes when prodded all the way through. Do not turn. Transfer to a hot serving platter; sprinkle with salt and pepper and 1 or 2 tablespoons lemon juice. Makes 6 to 8 servings.

Lemon Cream Cheese Tarts

3   eggs
3/4 cup sugar
2   teaspoons lemon peel, grated
1/2 cup lemon juice
1   large package (8 oz.) cream cheese at room temperature
6   baked tart shells (each about 2-1/2 inches diameter)

In top of double boiler, beat eggs to blend with sugar. Stir in lemon peel and juice and place over hot water. Cook until thick, stirring constantly. Mash cream cheese with a fork and gradually, smoothly beat in lemon sauce. Spoon into baked tart shells. Chill. Makes 6 servings.

North Beach Style Dinner

ANTIPASTO SANDWICH BOARD:

FRENCH BREAD   BUTTER   TUNA

SWEET ROASTED PEPPERS

FONTINA CHEESE

EGGPLANT WITH MOZZARELLA CHEESE

BROWN RICE

GREEN SALAD

ANCHOVY AND GARLIC DRESSING

LIME ICE WITH CRENSHAW MELON

This dinner can be held ready to serve for several hours if guests are to arrive at an indefinite time. Start with a mellow red wine with the antipasto board and serve it right on through the meal; this is the place for a California burgundy.

Antipasto Sandwich Board

At dinner time, group on a large tray a loaf of bread to slice, a pot of butter, a dish of canned tuna, a small bowl of canned sweet roasted red peppers (or sliced canned pimientos), and a wedge of fontina cheese to cut. Invite guests to serve themselves; make open face sandwiches to eat out of hand, spreading bread with butter and combining the remaining foods as toppings.

Eggplant with Mozzarella Cheese

2   medium-sized eggplants (about 1 lb. each)
    All-purpose flour
2   eggs beaten with 4 tablespoons water
    Salad oil
    Meat sauce (recipe follows)
1   pound mozzarella cheese, sliced

Cut eggplant into lengthwise slices about 1/4 inch thick. Coat each slice with flour, shake off excess, and turn in egg mixture. Drain briefly and sauté in about 1/4-inch salad oil over medium-high heat until well browned and tender when pierced; use a large frying pan, adding oil as needed, and cook eggplant without crowding. When browned, drain on absorbant material.

Line the bottom of a shallow 3-1/2 to 4-quart casserole with about half the eggplant. Spoon half the meat sauce over the top, and cover it with about half the cheese. Repeat with a layer of eggplant, then meat sauce, and finish with cheese. Cover and chill until time to bake.

Bake uncovered in a 375° oven until bubbly; takes about 40 minutes. Serve hot or keep hot to 2 to 3 hours on an electric warming tray. Makes 8 servings.

Meat Sauce:

1-1/2   pounds lean ground beef
1-1/4   to 1-1/2 pounds Italian-style pork sausages, casings removed and thinly sliced
1   green pepper, seeded and finely chopped
2   medium-sized onions, chopped
1/2   pound mushrooms, chopped
1   can (about 1 lb.) whole or pear-shaped tomatoes
1   large can (15 oz.) tomato sauce
1   can (6 oz.) tomato paste

In a 4 to 5-quart saucepan break apart ground beef and add the pork sausage, green pepper, onions, and mushrooms.

Cook over high heat, stirring frequently, until beef has lost its pink color. Add tomatoes, tomato sauce, and tomato paste. Simmer rapidly, uncovered, until sauce is very thick; about 45 minutes. Stir frequently. Remove from heat and let stand undisturbed for a few minutes until fat rises to the surface, then skim it off and discard. Use sauce while hot or when cold; cover and chill for up to 4 days, or freeze.

Brown Rice

Prepare enough brown rice for 8 servings, following package directions. Stir in 3 to 4 tablespoons butter and serve hot or cover and keep warm up to 2 or 3 hours on an electric warming tray. Makes 8 servings.

Anchovy and Garlic Dressing

Finely chop 6 to 8 canned anchovy fillets; combine with 1 small clove minced or mashed garlic, 1/2 cup olive oil, and 1/3 cup wine vinegar. Mix well to blend before using. Use at once or cover and let stand at room temperature until ready to mix with greens. Makes about 3/4 cup dressing or enough for 2 to 3 quarts broken greens to serve 8.

Lime Ice with Crenshaw Melon

4   teaspoons grated lime peel (use green part only)
2   cups each water and sugar
3/4 cup lime juice, unstrained
1   medium-sized Crenshaw melon

Combine peel, water, and sugar; cover and chill at least 4 hours. Stir to blend and pour through a fine wire strainer; discard peel. Add lime juice to syrup. Pour in a shallow metal pan; freeze at 0° or colder until solid.

Remove from freezer and let stand until you can break ice into pieces with a wooden spoon. Pour into a large mixing bowl and continue to smash ice with wooden spoon into very small pieces. Beat slowly, then gradually at high speed until mixture is slushy and thick and smooth like heavy cake batter. Wrap and freeze.

Seed Crenshaw and cut in serving wedges; scoop an equal measure of lime ice onto each wedge. Makes 6 to 8 servings.

Dinner for Two

BLUE CHEESE DIP   VEGETABLE RELISHES

BROILED SKIRT STEAKS

SAUTÉD CHERRY TOMATOES

GOLDEN DELICIOUS APPLES

GRUYÉRE CHEESE

Fresh spring vegetables are used abundantly in this healthful meal for two. The zestful cheese sauce enhances both the salad dipping vegetables and the skirt steaks. Plan to mix and chill cheese dip first. Cut vegetable relishes and refrigerate them. While the skirt steaks broil, sauté 1-1/2 cups cherry tomatoes, uncovered, in 2 teaspoons butter. Season with salt and pepper.

Blue Cheese Dip

1   small package (3 oz.) cream cheese
2   ounces (1/4 cup) blue cheese
1   tablespoon each finely chopped green onion and parsley
1/2 teaspoon each Worcestershire and prepared horseradish
1/2 teaspoon garlic salt
1/3 cup unflavored yogurt
4   or 5 mushrooms, sliced
1   zucchini, sliced
1   carrot, sliced

Beat together the cream cheese, blue cheese, green onion, parsley, Worcestershire, horseradish, garlic salt, and yogurt. Spoon into a bowl, cover, chill.

Serve half the sauce with the mushrooms, zucchini, and carrot. Save the rest for skirt steaks. Makes about 1 cup sauce.

Broiled Skirt Steaks

Buy 2 skirt steaks, untenderized, wrapped in a pinwheel, and skewered (about 6 ounces each). Place on a rack in a broiler pan and broil about 4 inches from the heat in a preheated broiler, turning once and allowing about 5 to 7 minutes to a side for rare meat. Season with salt and pepper. Serve with cheese dip. Makes 2 servings.

Grilled Ham Steak

BUTTER LETTUCE AND

CHERRY TOMATO HALVES

OIL AND VINEGAR DRESSING

GRILLED HAM STEAK WITH
CANTALOUPE AND PINEAPPLE

CHILE AND CHEESE RICE

CHOCOLATE COCONUT SUNDAES

An easy idea for serving family or a few guests without much work is to fix a thick ham steak right from the barbecue or oven broiler. This particular ham steak is served with a light glaze accompanied by wedges of fresh cantaloupe and slices of ripe pineapple that have been basted and barbecued until glazed. Serve them with a rice and cheese casserole which cooks only 30 minutes and can bake in the oven and be held on a warming tray while the meat finishes cooking on the grill.

Use a spicy oil and vinegar dressing on the bowl of lettuce and cherry tomato halves, using either your own recipe or bottled dressing. For the chocolate coconut sundaes, toast about 1/2 cup coconut and prepare your favorite chocolate sauce or purchase one to serve over vanilla ice cream. All preparation and cooking can be done within one hour.

Ham with Cantaloupe and Pineapple

       2   tablespoons melted butter or margarine
       3   tablespoons honey
     1/4   cup lime juice
            Dash nutmeg
   2-1/2   pound center slice of fully cooked ham (1 to
            1-1/2-inches thick)
       1   cantaloupe
       1   ripe pineapple

Combine in a small saucepan the melted butter, honey, lime juice and dash of nutmeg for a basting sauce. Heat, stirring until blended. Set aside; reheat before using.

Slash the outer layer of fat (at about 2-inch intervals) on the ham. Cut cantaloupe into 6 wedges; remove seeds and peel. Also cut 6 slices (about 3/4-inch thick)

from the ripe pineapple; peel, but leave core in place for easier handling.

To cook, brush both sides of ham steak with basting sauce. Place steak on a grill about 6 inches above medium-hot coals. Cook for 16 to 20 minutes, turning occasionally and basting frequently with the basting sauce. About 8 to 10 minutes before ham is done, brush melon and pineapple with basting sauce; place on grill. Cook fruit, turning and basting often, until glazed and lightly browned on all sides, about 10 minutes. To serve, arrange ham and fruits on carving board. Cut thin slices across the grain of meat. Makes 6 servings.

Chile and Cheese Rice

       1   cup long grain rice
            Boiling, salted water
       1   can (4 oz.) whole California green chiles, seeded and
            diced
   1-1/3   cups sour cream
     1/2   pound jack cheese, shredded (about 2 cups)

Cook rice in boiling water according to package directions. Combine the cooked rice, chiles, sour cream, and 1-1/2 cups of the cheese. Turn into a greased 1-1/2-quart casserole; sprinkle remaining cheese on top. Bake, uncovered, in a 350° oven for about 30 minutes or until cheese is bubbly and rice is heated through. Makes 6 servings.

Pork Chop Supper

BRAISED SMOKED PORK CHOPS

PINK GRAPEFRUIT ICE

ASPARAGUS SPEARS   EGGS IN SHELLS

CROISSANTS OR BRIOCHE

The grapefruit ice can be made as much as a week ahead eliminating last-minute preparation. You just need to braise the pork chops about 20 minutes. Soft-cook the eggs in their shells the last few minutes before serving. Allow 1 or 2 eggs for each serving. Prepare 2 packages frozen asparagus spears according to package directions. Warm croissants or brioche, frozen, from a bakery, or from your own recipe, in the oven.

Braised Smoked Pork Chops

In a large frying pan, arrange side by side 4 to 6 smoked loin pork chops, each cut about 3/4-inch thick. Add 3 tablespoons water; bring to simmer and cook over moderately-low heat, covered, until liquid is evaporated. Turn chops and add another 3 tablespoons water and cook, covered, until it is evaporated.

Add 2 more tablespoons water and stir free any browned particles, then cook, uncovered, until chops are lightly browned on one side. Turn chops and add another 2 tablespoons water, stirring free browned particles; cook until remaining sides are brown (about 20 minutes). Makes 4 to 6 servings.

Pink Grapefruit Ice

Grate 1 tablespoon pink grapefruit peel (use only the yellow, avoiding the white part of the skin) and mix with 1-1/2 cups sugar and 1 cup water. Cover and chill at least 4 hours or overnight. Stir to blend and pour through a fine wire strainer; discard peel. Add to syrup 2 cups freshly squeezed pink grapefruit juice. Tint it pale pink, if desired, with a few drops red food coloring. Pour mixture into a shallow metal pan; freeze at 0° or colder until solid.

Remove from freezer and let stand until you can break ice into chunks with a wooden spoon; pour into a large mixing bowl and continue to mash with spoon until pieces are very small. Beat slowly with mixer, then gradually turn speed to high and beat until ice is slushy, thick, and smooth like heavy cake batter. Wrap and freeze. To serve, let soften at room temperature for about 5 minutes, then scoop into bowls. Makes 6 servings.

Autumn Fireside Supper

SMOKED OYSTER SALAD PLATE

VEAL PICCATTA   ARTICHOKE HEARTS

HOT ROLLS   BUTTER

COMICE PEARS WITH
CHOCOLATE WHIPPED CREAM

This special intimate dinner is completely prepared at the last minute; it's ideal after a busy day.

Smoked Oyster Salad

Romaine lettuce leaves
6   *to 8 cherry tomatoes*
8   *thin cucumber slices*
1   *small can (8 oz.) smoked oysters*
    Oil and vinegar dressing

For each serving cover a salad plate with romaine leaves. Arrange on such plate 3 or 4 cherry tomatoes, 4 slices peeled cucumber, and half the smoked oysters. Dress with an oil and vinegar dressing made from your own recipe or a bottled one. Makes 2 servings.

Veal Piccatta

3/4   pound veal cutlet, cut 1/4-inch thick
1   tablespoon flour
1/2   teaspoon salt
1/8   teaspoon pepper
2   tablespoons butter
1/3   cup dry white wine
1   teaspoon grated lemon peel from 1/2 lemon
1   tablespoon butter
    Lemon slices

Place veal between 2 sheets waxed paper and pound with the smooth side of a mallet until meat is 1/8-inch thick. Cut meat into strips about 1-1/2-inch wide and 3 inches long. Remove any outer membrane. Lightly dust meat with flour and season with salt and pepper. Melt the 2 tablespoons butter in a large frying pan over medium-high heat, add meat, and sauté quickly, turning to brown both sides. (It takes about 4 minutes.)

Remove to a hot platter. Pour 1/3 cup dry white wine into the drippings and bring to a boil, scraping them up. Grate the lemon peel and add to pan along with the remaining tablespoon butter and heat until melted. Spoon sauce over veal and serve with lemon slices. Makes 2 servings.

Pears with Chocolate Whipped Cream

1/2   cup whipping cream
4   teaspoons ground sweet chocolate
1-1/2   teaspoons each powdered sugar and orange-flavored liqueur or undiluted frozen orange juice concentrate (thawed)
2   Comice pears, peeled, sliced, and cored

In a bowl combine the whipping cream, sweet chocolate, powdered sugar, and liqueur or orange juice concentrate. Beat until stiff. Cover and chill until serving time. Place pear slices in dessert bowls with tips pointing out and fill centers with cream. Makes 2 servings.

Soup Supper

LAMB SHANK BORSCHT

SOUR CREAM WITH DILL WEED

CRUSTY RYE BREAD   SWEET BUTTER

BUTTER LETTUCE SALAD

WINESAP OR GOLDEN DELICIOUS APPLES

SHARP CHEDDAR CHEESE

Only a few simple accompaniments are needed to turn this hearty, whole-meal soup into a satisfying feast. If you cook the lamb shanks a day ahead, cover and refrigerate the stock overnight. Before serving, skim off fat and simmer vegetables in lean stock while assembling the rest of the meal. Add sour cream and dill weed to each bowl of soup, if desired. For the salad, mix butter lettuce with your favorite homemade oil and vinegar dressing or purchased one.

Lamb Shank Borscht

6   lamb shanks, whole or cracked
1   can (1 lb. 15 oz.) chicken broth
1-1/2   cups water
1   bay leaf
6   whole black peppers
1   teaspoon salt
1   small green pepper, seeded and diced
3   medium-sized carrots, diced
1   medium-sized onion, finely chopped
4   small beets, diced
4   cups finely shredded cabbage
1   small potato, diced
2   tablespoons lemon juice
    Lemon wedges (optional)

Put lamb shanks, chicken broth, water, bay, black pepper, and salt in a large soup kettle or Dutch oven. Cover and simmer until lamb is tender, about 2 hours. (At this point you can cool, cover, and refrigerate soup.) Skim fat; discard. Strain broth, discard black pepper and bay. Return shanks (or just the meat) to the stock, add green pepper, carrots, onion, beets, cabbage, and potato; simmer 15 to 20 minutes, or until vegetables are tender. Remove from heat; stir in lemon juice. Ladle lamb, vegetables, and broth into bowls. Garnish with lemon, if desired. Makes 6 servings.

Coffee Table Sausages

ASSORTED SAUSAGES

MUSTARD   HORSERADISH

BROWNED POTATO PUFFS

FRESH SPINACH SALAD

RAISIN BREAD PARTY PUDDING

Choose an assortment of fully cooked sausages (such as smoked sausage links, garlic frankfurters, or kielbasa) if you just plan to brown them over a fire in the fireplace. Or if you prefer, cook sausages in the kitchen and serve them on a warm platter ready to eat. Allow 2 or 3 for each person. Assemble pudding ingredients ahead of time and then fold in the egg whites just before baking.

Fresh Spinach Salad

3/4   pound (about 1 bunch) spinach
  6   to 8 ounces fresh bean sprouts, rinsed and drained
  1   can (5 oz.) water chestnuts, drained and sliced
  4   green onions, thinly sliced
1/4   cup each salad oil and white wine vinegar
  2   tablespoons catsup
      Salt and pepper
  8   slices bacon, fried and crumbled
  2   hard-cooked eggs, sliced

Remove stems from spinach and discard. Wash leaves well, pat dry, and break into bite-sized pieces. Combine the spinach, bean sprouts, water chestnuts, and onions; cover and refrigerate up to 4 hours.

Mix together salad oil, vinegar, catsup, and salt and pepper to taste. To serve, add bacon to the spinach mixture, pour over the dressing, and mix gently. Garnish with egg slices. Makes 6 to 8 servings.

Raisin Bread Pudding

  4   or 5 slices raisin bread
3/4   cup sugar
1-1/2 teaspoons grated lemon peel
  3   tablespoons lemon juice
1/3   cup melted butter or margarine
  3   eggs, separated
2/3   cup milk
      Whipping cream (optional)

Cut bread into 1/2-inch cubes; you should have 2-1/2 cups. In a large bowl, mix together the bread cubes, 1/4 cup of the sugar, lemon peel and juice, and butter. In another bowl, beat egg yolks until thick; stir in milk. Add egg yolk mixture to bread cubes and mix well. You can do this much an hour ahead.

Just before baking, beat egg whites until soft peaks form; gradually add remaining 1/2 cup sugar and beat until whites hold stiff peaks. Gently fold egg whites into bread mixture. Turn into a greased 1-1/2-quart shallow baking dish. Bake in a 350° oven for 35 to 40 minutes, or until set when touched in center, and richly browned. Serve immediately, topping with whipped cream if desired. Makes 6 servings.

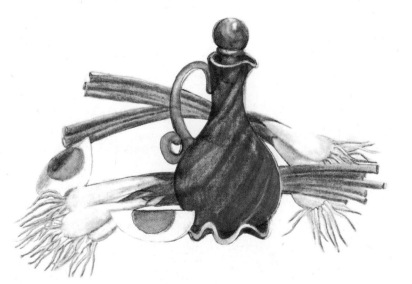

Index